Adventures in a Man's World

THE AUTHOR AT GLENWILD

SISTERS OF THE HUNT

Adventures in a Man's World

The Initiation of a Sportsman's Wife

COURTNEY BORDEN

(MRS. JOHN BORDEN)

FOREWORD BY MARY ZEISS STANGE

STACKPOLE
BOOKS

New foreword copyright © 2005 by Stackpole Books

Published by
STACKPOLE BOOKS
5067 Ritter Road
Mechanicsburg, PA 17055
www.stackpolebooks.com

Printed in the United States

First edition

10 9 8 7 6 5 4 3 2 1

Cover design by Tracy Patterson

Library of Congress Cataloging-in-Publication Data

Letts de Espil, Courtney.
    Adventures in a man's world / Courtney Borden ; foreword by Mary Zeiss Stange.
        p. cm.—(Sisters of the hunt)
    Originally published: New York : Macmillan Co., 1933.
    ISBN 0-8117-3205-3 (alk. paper)
    1. Hunting—Anecdotes. 2. Fishing—Anecdotes. 3. Letts de Espil, Courtney. I. Title.
II. Series.
    SK33.L47 2005
    799'082—dc22
                                                        2004057792

FOREWORD

As for the cold, are there many places in the world colder than a duck-blind on a raw November or December day when the skies are bursting with snow and the north wind whistles through you? I doubt it. I hazard even the Arctic because mukluks are cozy and warm, and feet in wet rubber boots for hours at a time are like icy appendages. In a duck-blind your nose feels as though it belonged to someone else, and your frost-bitten hands you rather wish were not part of the same person who a short while before stood by a warm fire, waiting for the morning coffee to boil.

—Courtney Borden[1]

How does it happen that a nice, upper-class city girl, born at the turn of the twentieth century and raised to expect a life of pampered luxury, finds herself shivering in a frigid Saskatchewan duck-blind? Outdoor writer George Reiger once hazarded a guess that the only reasons any female would want to venture into "the cold, wet realm in which ducks, dogs, and certain males seem to thrive" would be that either "by sharing a blind, a girl might make her father proud, or a young lady might find a husband like her own duck-hunting dad."[2] Like many another sportswoman who has spent the better part of countless days hunkered down with her shotgun amidst frosty reeds and rushes, Courtney Borden would surely have balked at the sexism underlying that statement. Yet, as she recounts in this fascinating little book, love did have something to do with it.

When twenty-five year-old Chicago socialite Courtney Louise Letts married John Borden—who headed the condensed milk company which bore his family name—in 1925, she probably assumed that a life of genteel domesticity, with the occasional lavish holiday, lay ahead of her. But as she recounts in the first chapter below, John Borden quickly set about shattering any illusions she may have nurtured about leisurely trans-Atlantic cruises and cosmopolitan vacations:

> "You may prefer trips to London, Paris, and the Riviera, but I don't," he had explained. "I would like to go there—once in a while—but vacations like that don't count. Most American men dislike being dragged 'abroad' every chance they have to get away." He had been serious. "I'd like to take you along—just to see how you will like this sort of thing . . . cold . . . getting up at dawn. . . . Because if you do—" He had stopped to consider what to add next. "I've always led that kind of life, you know."[3]

In addition to running what was then the largest food company in the United States, John Borden was by avocation an avid outdoorsman. As she tells it, his young bride faced a relatively simple choice. She could play the conventional wifely role of "audience," watching passively, whether her man was riding off with other men for a day's quail shooting, or sailing away for a months-long voyage above the Arctic circle. Or she could accept his invitation to join in the action, to—as she puts it on several occasions—prove that she could "make it," no matter how much that entailed in terms of discomfort, inconvenience, or (not infrequently) fear.

Courtney Borden approached her choice with enthusiasm, a level head, and an open mind. "It was going to be entirely different from anything I had ever tried before. It would be an experience, an insight into a man's world and why many husbands spend autumn week-ends away from home."[4] Whether upland bird shooting, waterfowling, unlocking the mysteries that seemed to bind together the fraternity of fly fishers, or—in the capstone adventure in her "initiation"—embarking on an Arctic cruise in quest of walrus, Alaskan brown bears, and polar bears, at each step along the way Borden took care to do her homework. She practiced her shooting; she read up on her quarry; she reminded herself that she was always a novice, yet nonetheless determined to "make it," whatever that took, and without complaint. Habitual diarist that she was, she kept copious notes detailing and digesting her experiences afield. These diaries formed the bases of her two hunting books: 1928's *The Cruise of the Northern Light*,[5] and the present volume, published five years later.

Of course, given their wealth and the circles in which they customarily moved, the Bordens frequently hunted in rather more luxurious circumstances than the average hunter, then or now, could imagine. One reviewer of *The Cruise of the Northern Light* wrote disparagingly that it was "the sea in silk pajamas."[6] Yet such criticism is not entirely fair to Borden. As the ensuing narrative amply attests, she endured her share of rough, rustic camping conditions, in which personal hygiene owed at best to a combination of ice-cold water and wishful thinking. She "made it" through rigorous hikes over rough terrain, weighed down by her gun and cumbersome hunting gear. She risked not only discomfort but personal injury in her increasingly ardent pursuit of game. At a climactic moment below, in this book's narrative of the Alaskan cruise, she would lead the other women aboard the *Northern Light* in arguing passionately, and with justice, that they had earned the right to hunt walrus along with the men.

Any woman who has come to hunting as an adult, and likely because of a man in her life (as have the majority of contemporary American women hunters[7]), will find that these themes strike a responsive chord. So, too, will Borden's not infrequent references to John's impatience with her, for not shooting well enough or fast enough, or his sometimes ill-concealed glee at an awkward situation she had gotten herself into. Some things never seem to change, and these remain familiar behavioral quirks, among even the most supportive sportsmen. Courtney Borden had a knack for responding with enviable equanimity, a "good sport" in every instance. A modern reader can only agree with the contemporary critic who wrote of this book and its author, "a woman who can shoot straight, grin when she misses, go head over heels down the rapids and bewail only the lost steelhead has proved that sport is by no means only a man's world."[8]

Another critic favorably remarked this book's "cheeky camaraderie," and the phrase aptly captures Borden's style.[9] In *The Cruise of the Northern Light* she had endeavored to present an accurate and objective log of the venture which was officially titled the "Borden Field Museum 1927 Alaska Arctic Expedition." In the present later work, which is more of a memoir, she writes freely and far more candidly, about the Alaskan expedition as well as about her various hunting experiences before and after that pivotal adventure. Borden was a keen observer of both nature and people. She can place the reader in a scene with sometimes startling immediacy, as for example when she recalls a particular autumn morning: "The out of doors, in all its flaming colors, was a veritable artists' paradise, more like a canvas in some gallery where a visitor might stand before it and comment incredulously: 'Nature *couldn't* be like that.'"[10] Her descriptions of persons are at once discerning and fresh, punctuated by cleverly honed metaphors—as when she depicts her duck-hunting guide Bill, "scanning the horizon with the same pleased appraisal as a drama critic employs when he studies the opening scene of a play and feels he is about to witness a fine production," or herself and other quail hunters searching the trees for a covey they have just flushed, "like gaping country-bumpkins on their first visit to the tall buildings of a city, craning our necks backward and gazing upwards for several minutes into the confusing branches."[11]

Borden's intense sensitivity to time and place lend historical depth to the narrative which follows. *Adventures in a Man's World* is a bracing collection of smartly crafted hunting stories, and well worth reading on that account alone. But, as a record of hunting in a particular time and place, the book ultimately aims to be rather more than that. The time is the onset of the Great Depression, and the place is rural America.

From the start, economic hard times form the background of her story. Early on, we read of Bill Brown, a market hunter turned hunting guide, who to his chagrin was forced to remove his youngest daughter from school to come home and work so that the family could scrape together the money for his cataract surgery. We read of "tramps, or hoboes" drifting by the Bordens' hunting camp, drawn by the comforting light of their gas lamps and the aroma of sizzling steaks and onions.

Of course, these people inhabited a very different world than did John Borden who, when he could not find a yacht to his liking for the Alaskan cruise, simply had one built, or his wife, who when confronted with yet another day's cold-water ablutions in camp yearned for soap and a bathtub—a jade bathtub, that is. Courtney Borden can at times be irksomely oblivious to the extent to which class privilege infuses her narrative, as when, shortly after noting the procession of hoboes past their camp, she rhapsodizes about the "greatest joy of camp-life" being that "there was no one to bother us," so that "we could indulge in a never-to-be-forgotten childish desire to mess about with dishes and frying pans and cooking of food."[12]

Yet it would be a mistake to confound such apparent unawareness with callousness. As her narrative develops, Borden sees, with increasing sharpness, the social consequences of the crumbling economy. She cannot evade the issue of difference among persons. Yet neither can she, inborn optimist that she apparently is, shake the conviction that there are things more precious than money that form the bedrock of social cohesion. And one of these things is the sporting life.

About three-quarters of the way through her story, Borden offers a kind of apology: "Perhaps I am leaving a wrong impression," she writes. "The impression that life, for us, has been one continual merry-go-round of sport—one continual search for this recreation or that adventure. Quite the contrary. These excursions into the refreshing peace of woods and waters have been our greatest luxuries." Especially, she continues, during the past three years. Consulting her ever-present journal, she explains, "In my notes I remarked, 'The deeper became the depression the more we trout-fished on Sundays.' " And, thanks to the "democracy of the fishing stream," she discovered a bond with other anglers, deeper than anything having to do with ties and lures, or with the accouterments of class:

> For I have seen and talked with unemployed men—unfortunate products of our machine civilization—their wives and children, who have sought during the past three summers the beautiful streams of Wisconsin and Michigan on the banks of which they have made camps and there lived happily for two and three months at a time. The father, his heart still in the cities where he hoped a job might soon be waiting, would periodically jump into his truck and "beat it," as one expressed himself, "back to the city to see what might be open," only to return and forget his fresh disappointment in the joyful casting of a fly."

In these men and women, in their "cheerful philosophy in the face of adversity, mingled with a sort of fierce pride in this great country itself," Borden reads a powerful lesson of faith and courage. It is, as well, "a lesson in the fellowship of humankind," grounded in a kind of natural democracy in action.[13]

Here Borden is tapping into a rich symbolic vein, which historians and sociologists of sport have only more recently set in the context of American social and environmental history. In his *Hunting and the American Imagination*, Daniel Justin Herman traces how national ideals of freedom and individual responsibility became encoded in the American notion of hunting as a "pastime for the democratic many," against the European idea of hunting as an activity reserved for the aristocratic few.[14] Along similar lines, Jan Dizard in *Mortal Stakes* characterizes the hunter as "protean Jeffersonian democrat," a minority in society it is true, but one which historically "was portrayed as and very probably felt that they were embodying values endorsed by the entire society."[15] These are the foundational American values that see people through when the going gets tough, and key among them is the idea—so firmly rooted as to be a conviction—of self-reliance.

Dizard studied late-twentieth-century hunters in the Northeast, some of whom offset unemployment and seasonal layoffs by hunting and fishing; this, he found, not only "took the edge off unemployment," it also gave them a "sense of control" in the face of economic disempowerment.[16] Borden would surely have recognized her fellow anglers in Dizard's analysis.

Herman also points out the direct relationship that existed historically between the rise of sport hunting and the creation of an ethic of stewardship: "Those Americans who call themselves environmentalists . . . do not have to be hunters to appreciate what nineteenth- and early twentieth-century sport hunters accomplished. Their love for American fauna, their fascination with natural history, and their appreciation for the sublime contributed to our own sensibilities."[17] It is this commingling of the aesthetic and the ethical that gave force and depth to Aldo Leopold's idea of the "land ethic."[18] And, as the Depression deepened and the need to escape its pressures intensified, this same sensibility apparently led John and Courtney Borden to relocate from their Chicago residence to Glenwild, a Mississippi cotton plantation and quail preserve they had acquired.

"Here," Borden writes, "we have come from the North to live quietly and calmly and appreciate the richness of each day as it moves inevitably from sun-up to sun-down, in a leisurely fashion so easy to enjoy."[19] It is clear from her effusive descriptions of the romance of the Southland that Borden has, quite literally, bought into another powerful cultural mythology: one which, again, had everything to do with sporting activities. As ethnographer Stuart Marks has argued, there is a powerful irony in the fact that traditions of "Southern gentility" were often not only accepted but actually perpetuated by Northerners who acquired plantation properties during the late nineteenth and early twentieth centuries. This was particularly true when it came to the rites of quail hunting. According to Marks,

> Quail are the stuff of Southern traditions. The pursuit of quail is linked in the myth of the Southern gentleman whose land ownership is his source of wealth, prestige, and independence. The fidelity of quail to place . . . their response to habitat improvements and to stewardship . . . their pursuit with special breeds of dogs (pointers and setters) that "honor" each other's points . . . their sudden bursts into flight . . . and their cockiness and pronouncements of presence (they whistle their own names!) are some of the characteristics seized upon to construct

durable structures of emotion and ritual. The irony is that
the prestige of quail hunting is of recent vintage and one
in which Yankee wealth played a large, creative role.[20]

Glenwild is a case in point. Marks suggests that to assert one's identity as a quail hunter is to "lay claim to a genealogy of status and control over the good stuff of life."[21] But this "stuff" must be judiciously managed.

By the time John Borden acquired Glenwild, its population of quail was in decline. Bringing the birds back, as Courtney Borden explains in the appendix to this volume, entailed striking an ecological balance between cotton farming and wildlife management. That, in turn, meant returning to older, more primitive ways of farming. It turns out that the measures she describes in the appendix were quite forward-looking for their time. As Marks explains, "In the past, quail thrived when and where the land was hand and mule worked, the countryside was crisscrossed with overgrown ditches, and fence rows provided cover between the fields. Modern intensive farming with its pulpwood, pasture, intensive crop plantings, cleaned fields, and chemicals have reduced much of the habitat containing the birds' needs."[22] The Glenwild project was to restore that habitat.

In a sense, of course—and this is part of the mythic appeal of the enterprise—restoring the quail meant restoring the cultural ambience of the post–Civil War South. Whereas formerly the land had been worked by slaves, the labor was now done by tenant farmers both black and white. But it was done in the traditional ways, and workers likely lived in physical conditions not terribly different from those of their forebears.

Borden's descriptions of these conditions ooze with the romance of the Southland, as perhaps only a transplanted Northerner could convey it. By day, "Negro cabins dotted here and there, offered us their porches overflowing with laughing children and their yards with chickens, stray dogs, and an occasional hog. Crops were picked so the fields were bare of yield."[23] When darkness falls, however, the cabins appear "most mysterious."

> No children stood on the porches now and waved to us,
> for through the windows shone the fitful pinkish glow of
> a fire on every hearth. And as we rode by we glanced
> within and saw a roomful of black faces, black heads,
> black forms—all sizes—silhouetted against the walls
> where a reflection of red flames danced. Close to the fire
> they sat, munching on their frugal meal.[24]

She goes on to describe it all as a scene of "great peace and contentment," with an admittedly embarrassing allusion to Gershwin's *Porgy*. Stereotypes aside, however, it is nonetheless, for its time, a sympathetic and humanizing picture; here, as elsewhere in her writing, Borden displays far less overt racism than most of her contemporaries.

Her descriptions of the living circumstances of "poor whites" are similar. However, interestingly, she sees persons of her own race more distinctly in light of the Depression:

> A few years ago my heart would have ached at the sight of those dilapidated little homes and the barefoot mothers and fathers and children whom we passed in the fields. But this day I could hardly feel the same way. They had a house to live in, they had a huge fat hog wallowing in a small enclosure behind the chicken coop where a rooster and five or six hens strutted in the sunlight, they had a mule to work their cash crop of cotton and corn, they had sorghum for molasses, and a garden on each side of the house. Children were thin but their voices held the unmistakable ring of happiness, they had a dog or two, and perhaps a young wiggly kitten for playmates. The sun was warm on bare little legs and arms and hair that had perhaps never been confined by a hat. This sun gave them what health they had, the sun and clean air.[25]

She goes on to infer that these backcountry folk are better off than their counterparts in the "jangling skyscraper city," where there were "not enough jobs and homes for all."[26]

It is unlikely that anyone so ensconced in the class privilege conveyed by ownership of a plantation could witness the scenes of poverty Borden describes absent the romanticized myth of the Southland that would, a few years later, make Margaret Mitchell's *Gone with the Wind* a bestseller on both sides of the Mason-Dixon Line. Nonetheless, the narrative she develops in the final two chapters of *Adventures in a Man's World* provides a most valuable glimpse into this particular moment in America's cultural history.

As things turned out, for Borden herself the idyllic plantation life, and beyond that the adventurous lifestyle, she describes with such obvious enjoyment in this book proved to be fleeting. There is a hint at one point that she is narrating a life she is perhaps already coming to see as a thing of the past. She writes:

. . . when realizing that after writing all these stories of birds and game I have not once mentioned how truly funny the racket of firearms and gunning and ammunition can seem, I decide I was dull to have taken it all so seriously. For I did mean to laugh at it more, since it can produce many chuckles, outwardly and inwardly, when the struggle is over and only memories remain. But there is reason why I wrote so solemnly. Because—when the impact of each new experience was actually taking place—it *was* serious! Terribly so. Grimly serious.[27]

The Bordens divorced in 1933, the same year this book was published. Courtney subsequently married Felipe Espil, then the Argentine ambassador to the United States, and embarked on yet another round of adventures "in a man's world," this time the one of politics and diplomacy. The diaries she kept between 1933 and 1953 are generally regarded by historians as valuable resources chronicling life in Washington during the Roosevelt administrations.[28] Borden never achieved the publication she sought for them, and they are today housed in the Library of Congress, Manuscript Collection.

Courtney Borden also published two books in Spanish—*La Esposa del Embajador* (1967) and *Noticias Confidenciales de Buenos Aires a USA* (1969)—about her experiences during her husband's diplomatic postings in Madrid and Sao Paolo and life in Argentina under Juan Peron. After Espil's death, she settled in New York City and remarried.

Courtney Letts Borden de Espil Adams died at the age of ninety-five in 1995.

Mary Zeiss Stange
Ekalaka, Montana
August 2004

NOTES

1. See below, 30–31.
2. George Reiger, "Instinct and Reality," *Field and Stream* (September 1991), 16.
3. Below, 3–4.
4. Below, 3. Her remark about "many husbands" is no exaggeration; at the time Borden was writing, owing to a variety of social and economic factors, the number of Americans hunting was growing exponentially. By 1945, one in four American men was a sport hunter. See James Swan, *In Defense of Hunting* (San Francisco: HarperSanFrancisco, 1995), 2–3; and Daniel Justin Herman, *Hunting and the American Imagination* (Washington and London: Smithsonian Institution Press, 2001), 270–271.
5. Another volume in the Sisters of the Hunt series.
6. Arthur Warren, writing in *The Nation* (December 26, 1928). Quoted in Kenneth P. Czech, *With Rifle and Petticoat: Women as Big Game Hunters, 1880–1940* (Lanham, Maryland: The Derrydale Press, 2002), 102.
7. While the social pattern seems to be gradually changing, it remains the case that most women who hunt started because of men in their lives—husbands, boyfriends, male friends—and as teenagers or adults, rather than as children. On the implications of the different ways women approach hunting than do men, who have conventionally been introduced to it as boys, see Mary Zeiss Stange and Carol K. Oyster, *Gun Women: Firearms and Feminism in Contemporary America* (New York: New York University Press, 2000), Chapter 4, "Babies and Bullets in the Same Conversation."
8. Paul Allen, in *Book* (February 19, 1933), 10. Quoted in Czech, 103.
9. Review in the *Boston Transcript* (March 25, 1933), 1. Quoted in Czech, 103.
10. Below, 45.
11. Below, 31–32, 220.
12. Below, 30.
13. Below, 186–188.
14. Daniel Justin Herman, *Hunting and the American Imagination*. See especially chapter 16, "Manly Men and Manly Women," 218–236.
15. Jan E. Dizard, *Mortal Stakes: Hunters and Hunting in Contemporary America* (Amherst and Boston: University of Massachusetts Press, 2003), 42. On the broad idea of the hunter embodying the values of the larger society, see also the works of Paul Shepard, particularly *The*

Tender Carnivore and the Sacred Game (New York: Charles Scribner's Sons, 1973) and *Coming Home to the Pleistocene*, Edited by Florence R. Shepard (Washington: Island Press/Shearwater Books, 1998); James Swan, *In Defense of Hunting*; and Mary Zeiss Stange, *Woman the Hunter* (Boston: Beacon Press, 1997).

16. Dizard, 93.
17. Herman, 280. On the relationship between sport hunting and environmental stewardship, see especially John F. Reiger, *American Sportsmen and the Origins of Conservation*, Third Edition, revised and expanded (Corvallis: Oregon State University Press, 2001); and James A. Tober, *Who Owns the Wildlife? The Political Economy of Conservation in Nineteenth-Century America* (Westport, CT: Greenwood Press, 1981).
18. One of the most important figures in the history of conservation in America, Aldo Leopold (1887–1948) is widely regarded as the father of wildlife ecology. See his *A Sand County Almanac* (New York: Ballantine Books, 1966; originally published by Oxford University Press in 1949), particularly the essay titled "The Land Ethic."
19. Below, 203.
20. Stuart A. Marks, *Southern Hunting in Black and White: Nature, History, and Ritual in a Carolina Community* (Princeton: Princeton University Press, 1991), 170. While Marks's work is based on ethnography he did in a North Carolina county, his generalized conclusions about Southern life and culture readily translate to the Mississippi context. For another illuminating description of the rituals of Southern quail hunting, this one set in Georgia, see Jimmy Carter, *An Outdoor Journal: Adventures and Reflections* (New York: Batnam Books, 1988), "The Prince of Game Birds," 153–169.
21. Marks, 173. Indicating that Southern quail hunting continues to be a powerful marker of wealth and status, the September 2004 issue of *Sports Afield* features an article about "tasting the good life at the South's best quail plantations." According to the author, "For the most part, wild-bird plantation hunting is not available to the public in this region unless one is an invited guest or willing to purchase fifteen- or thirty-day blocks of time at twelve thousand dollars a day for the hunt and accommodations on one of the wild-bird plantations." The only nonwhite faces in the photographs accompanying the article are those of the grooms handling the hunters' horses. See Dale C. Spartas, "Southern Tradition," *Sports Afield* (September 2004), 64–69. In this connection it is interesting to note that Jimmy Carter, in the

essay cited above, remarks that it was only after he became Governor of Georgia, and later President of the United States, that he was "invited to enjoy the beautiful pageantry of the large plantations . . . whose prime reason for existence was quail hunting," *An Outdoor Journal*, 159.
22. Marks, 173.
23. Below, 212.
24. Below, 215–216.
25. Below, 224–225.
26. Below, 226.
27. Below, 169.
28. See "Family Papers of Male Diplomats: Manuscript Division," Library of Congress web site, http://memory.loc.gov/ammem/awh-html/awmss5/male_diplo.html.

TO
MY MOTHER
CORA PERKINS LETTS
WITH MY LOVE

The Time has Come, My Husband Said
To Follow Other Trails
For Ducks and Trout and Polar Bears
And Partridges and Quails

CONTENTS

AUTUMN

SPRING

SUMMER

LATE SUMMER

WINTER

AUTUMN

I

Canvas-Back and Sharp-Tailed Grouse

A BEGINNING

"Do you think you might enjoy it?" he had said, before answering the invitation.

The white dawn lifted slowly. Saskatchewan seemed to be an immense sea of wheat fields. They engulfed the little car as it sped along the dirt road, a cloud of black dust whirling behind. The wheat had been garnered from the great fields, stubble sprinkled with frost glistened in the increasing light.

It was going to be entirely different from anything I had ever tried before. It would be an experience, an insight into a man's world and why many husbands spend autumn week-ends away from home.

"You may prefer trips to London, Paris, and the Riviera, but I don't," he had explained. "I would like to go there—once in a while—but vacations like that don't count. Most American men dislike being dragged 'abroad' every chance they have to get away." He had been serious. "I'd like to take you along—just to see how you will like this sort of thing . . . cold . . . getting up at

3

dawn. . . . Because if you do—" He had stopped to consider what to add next. "I've always led that kind of a life, you know."

We were passing small, isolated houses and barns. Farmers were commencing to move about their muddy yards. Cocks were crowing. On the left an enormous mass of crows rose out of the wheat stubble, now golden in the morning sun, and also a small flock of wild duck.

The driver turned in his seat. "Buffalo Lake is over there," he commented interestedly, and pointed one finger, "about three more miles." Buffalo Lake was our destination. We were going there to visit Wm. B. Mershon at his shooting lodge, Assiniboine House.

Four o'clock had indeed been a cold and early moment to be dragged off a train. When the porter knocked it had been as black as night beyond the green shades. The station at Moose Jaw was equally black, and windy. "Good duck day," John had commented as we turned over our luggage to a polite red cap. No matter how early the hour a person receives courteous and immediate attention when travelling anywhere in Canada. We had recently enjoyed a few days of fishing for King salmon in the beautiful blue bays off Victoria. We were already admirers of Canadian railroads, hotels, taxi-drivers, fishermen and guides.

"You'll get an extra good breakfast, sir, on that corner opposite the station," the red cap had suggested. "I'll watch your bags."

All of this service did make four-fifteen seem more bearable. Anyway, why fuss over being awakened from sleep at such an hour! All good duck hunters always rise before dawn. This I knew.

Our breakfast turned out to be surprisingly good, and most welcome. While waiting for pancakes to rise, my husband had wandered off somewhere to purchase cigarettes. I visited a nearby drug store in search of a supply of outdoor magazines. Reappearing with *Outdoor Life, Outdoor America, National Sportsman, Field and Stream,* under my arm, I found my travelling companion making a considerable dent in a platter of steaming buckwheat cakes. "You should be flattered," he teased, with a laugh, as I joined him. "When I returned with my cigarettes the woman at the counter called to me, 'Say,' she said, 'your girl-friend told me to tell you she'd be back in a minute.'"

All these things I was remembering as we covered the last three miles. Wives, evidently, weren't expected to be having breakfast in a restaurant at four-fifteen! After rounding a sharp curve, we suddenly came upon a one-storied frame lodge.

This was Assiniboine House. It perched on the edge of a low bluff, looking out upon Buffalo Lake. Smoke poured out of the one chimney. It was a friendly, welcome sort of place.

"Here we are!" smiled the driver. Glancing over the lake we could see ducks in the air; in twos and threes, singles, and larger numbers in flight formation. Down the center of the lake they flew. There was something thrilling and beautiful about those wild birds, and the sounds of their calling. The romance of their flight suggested far away ice-fields over which they had come, southern rice fields to which they would go when winter came.

Just then the door opened. Four men, our host and three grey-haired guests were there to greet us.

"Hello!" They called cheerily. "We're just having breakfast. How about a cup of coffee?"

On the glassed-in porch hung several brace of canvas-back, mallards, ruddies, green-winged and blue-winged teal. But to me they were just ducks, different kinds of wild ducks.

"Pretty good, eh?" one man chuckled, rubbing his hands while he enjoyed the pleasant memory of the sport the game had offered. "Do you shoot?" he turned and addressed me. Then his face registered surprise. . . . "No? . . . My daughter does—well, too."

Within the low ceilinged, warm building a huge fire crackled on the hearth and there was coffee in a pot on the table, bacon, and waffles. "We've been lazy this morning, waiting for you," Mr. Mershon said.

Soon we were climbing into a small boat loaded with shell boxes, guns, wooden decoys, dog, four human beings, one live decoy, and a box containing lunch. It was all exciting, the eager preparation and planning, the heated duck-and-gun-and-shell conversation, and now the choppy blue waves over which we putt-putted towards the low-lying opposite shore. Beside me, on the same seat, crouched the big black dog, a Labrador retriever. Her funny wise face lifted up into the wind. Her black ears, lined with delicate pink the color of the inside of a shell, blew with the breeze that she sniffed, while her strong body trembled with both nerves and excitement. She was like a ballet dancer, on her toes to the first strains from the orchestra.

The three men discussed the distinctive merits of guns and shells. I do not now recall what our host carried, but John's was a twenty-gauge L. C. Smith, thirty inch, full choke in both barrels; with number six shot, extra long range duckload.

On a flat point of land jutting out into the water a brush blind had been constructed. While the two hunters settled themselves in it, and George, the "pusher," laid out with infinite pains the complicated pattern of wooded blocks, hundreds of ducks filled the sky. We could hear their loud calls from every side. The wind caused the blocks to bob up and down, rising and falling like live birds. Our flier had been fastened to a log and had begun at once her busy quack-quack.

We were ready. The audience and dog hid themselves beyond a scrub bush behind the men, and sat very still. The two hunters, and their pusher now holding on to the live hen by a string, were seated well up in front.

"Mark right! . . ." hissed George.

Four shots, both barrels of two guns. Three ducks fell. I wanted to shout "Good shot!" but decided better not.

"Mark left!" . . . cried the pusher and this time he tossed out the live hen quacking frantically until she lit on the crest of the waves. This accomplished the hoped-for result. The wild fowl saw her, and heard her. Round the blind they circled—but, suddenly, up they swung and away they flew.

"What's the matter?" demanded John, peering behind him towards the bush. "Keep your head down. Your hat's too light!"

Hundreds of duck whizzed past the blind but

too far out on the lake to be within range. The speed of the canvas-back was for me something amazing, wary fowl, making, they say, seventy miles per hour. Flying to windward, spying the decoys and the "flier," they would now and then work up to leeward of the guns. But more often they would sail by at high speed.

Flirt crouched obedient and quiet, waiting for her orders to retrieve those birds floating on their back with the current. Each time the guns blazed she shivered with anticipation, and when one plopped into the water nearby she would rise to a sitting position, and then hopefully lick her chops. Each time that she heard "Mark right! . . . Behind! . . . Mark left! . . ." her ears would stand straight up and her alert eyes would follow the swift wings in the air. Thrice she nuzzled up to me, and whined, wanting to know when I thought her chance would come.

The two guns were well up to their mark. They would take their limits before very long. It was thrilling, being there, even though you were nothing more than audience! The flight of the birds, the fall sky, the bracing wind, and the keenness and sportsmanship of the black dog as she threw herself headlong into the cold choppy waves and swam back, one bird in her mouth at a time, was all quite different from anything I had ever witnessed. The dog, with game in her mouth, made me think of covers on outdoor magazines, of old prints, of illustrations in books.

Finally growing more or less numb with cold, and from lack of being able to stamp up and down, I began to turn over in my mind the disturbing thought of the guest on the porch who had that morning commented with surprise, "No? . . . My daughter does—well, too." At this very moment the three men in the fore part of our blind were not bothering in the least about the cold. They were completely engrossed in themselves and the pleasure of their sport. They were lost in it, forgetful of me, and of everything else in the world save the joys of the present. Men were odd things. They apparently had the ability to shut out all else—excepting that which they were doing at the moment. This must be the reason why they play all games better than we do? They can thrust aside past and future and immediate worries, enjoy the hour to its full. More sensible creatures than we are.

I recalled also the preceding December and January, during the week-ends of my first winter at the Plantation when the men rode out into the sedge and cotton fields behind Minnie and Girlie and all the other hunting dogs. What fun they had had, shooting or missing the fast-flying quail, and laughing over their mistakes when the day was done. And how stupid it had been after the first time or two—to follow behind and be left waiting on a hillside with the colored boy and the horses while the men gaily trudged away in search of singles! Often we lookers-on had to stand, or sit our horses, for an hour or more, listening to vague shots from somewhere in the deep woods or red gullies. But what could you do about it if you did not know a rifle from a shot-gun, or how to handle either? Perhaps Mister So and So's daughter had been smarter than I had at first given her credit. . . . And he was proud of her.

*   *   *   *

The second day we were to go in search of sharp-tailed grouse, and not ducks. In a car fortunately accustomed to much punishment we bumped over miles and miles of black mud roads, for we were well back in the country, searching on either side for likely-looking stubble. Then parking at the side of the road, and clambering out, we would start across the broad flat fields. But we took no dog. "Better to scare them up yourself rather than permit a dog to run them up long before the guns get in range," our host had explained as his theory. The birds were wild, having been shot at by many hunters, but fortunately

11

were found in the open and when once under way flew fairly straight.

Expecting only canvas-back shooting John had not brought with him a field gun. Nevertheless, by the time we sat down under a grove of autumn-tinted trees for rest and a quick bite of lunch that we had brought in the car, he and Mr. Mershon had enjoyed considerable success. The shooting had been good, birds plentiful, and hunters up to their mark.

But of all this initiation into duck and grouse shooting, I remember most keenly the evenings in company with the four seasoned sportsmen, feeling their, and John's, healthful enjoyance of the long days spent in the open. From desks and long business hours they had broken away to get a much-needed, much appreciated relaxation. And they had found it. No one appeared to possess a worldly care, nor a worldly contact. While we sat in the cheery main room of the little lodge, waiting hungrily for dinner on that first night, our host broiled a huge, juicy, wonderful smelling steak on a spit before the blazing logs; and on the second evening carved with exquisite precision a fifteen pound home-grown turkey which he himself had basted, stuffed, and roasted. This was all part—if not the greater part—of the day's pleasure. Women, somehow, I decided, miss much in life that is worth while. In search of bigger things we overlook small, simple pleasures.

Afterwards, seated round the table, two stout candles sputtering in the center, one person became a charmed listener to further tales of men and dogs and ducks and guns. Our host, sportsman and naturalist, author of several published volumes on wild-life, contributed observations as enchanting as any of Hudson's stories. Here was a sparkling breath of freedom from cities, where I had always lived, here was knowledge and a slice of life to be envied.

The listener there and then decided that despite the risk of being for many years a novice, and even a nuisance, if she were invited again she would not accept merely as *audience*. "I've always led that kind of a life," *he* had said.

II

Mallards and Slim Bean's Slough

A YEAR LATER guns had become a daily part of our conversation. And after a few trials at clay pigeons it was decided I might go along for a mallard shoot on the Illinois River, as partner and not audience.

Browning, where we were bound, would have meant either an uncomfortable night trip by train, or seven or eight hours by motor. We chose the latter. The farm lands which we passed with their miles and miles of corn and wheat, reminded me of the vast wheat fields of Saskatchewan. We were engulfed by them in Illinois, in the same way in which we had been in Canada. There were no trees, except those along the road in the humble and peaceful communities with fitting names such as *Mossville*. Here lay the scenes of the Spoon River Anthology. Here stretched on all sides the financial wherewithal belonging to farmers whose combined vote has for long been coveted by each would-be President of the United States.

The road for several miles was lined by poplars, reminiscent of a lovely poplared highway in France, leading north out of *Bar le Duc*. Only here there would be no *brioche* to be enjoyed at a small round table under a spreading umbrella in any of the small towns, no *vin ordinaire*. There was, instead, dinner in a cafeteria at Peoria, an imposing dinner in many thick white dishes on a square tin tray. We were travelling, not in France, but in rural America.

Bill Brown's small frame house loomed warm and inviting when we, tired and dusty, drew up to it at ten o'clock. A light blazed forth from a curtained window where in true small-town fashion the shade had not been drawn.

We honked the horn. Then we commenced unloading the luggage. In another minute we heard a big voice boom out: "I just finished tellin' Carl he ought t' find a car and see if you folks were mired up somewhare. That there slippery mud between here and Beardstown's 'nough to mire up any car."

Bill was with us: an enormous man with the top of his head bald and thick glasses covering his kindly old eyes.

"I told th' boys it's lucky you folks come this week," he continued, as he assisted in carrying our belongings to the house. "The mallards are comin' in thick and Carl and I've signed up Slim Bean's slough for Saturday and Sunday. Ought to be mighty fair shootin'."

Bill Brown had been for over forty years, first the best known market hunter on the Illinois River in the early days, and later pusher for a prominent club. There is still no one on the River who understands better the habits of wild fowl; and no one who has a better stock of ready-made tales of flights of ducks, and hunting incidents, with which to entertain the bored hunter when birds are not flying.

Now that he has no other job, he and his wife make a few honest dollars boarding hunters during the duck season. The shorter the season the less they make. His wife and sons and daughter shove their beds into a rear bedroom of their small house—visitors never know exactly where—while Old Bill himself catches a series of short naps on a bench in the living room. It is fairly certain that he sleeps with both eyes open watching for his time piece to tell him that four o'clock has arrived. Others might over-sleep. But not he! Wild ducks would be flying.

We were given an enormous hot dinner. It slipped down pleasantly after two cold hours spent in a ditch where we had been "mired up" as Bill so ably expressed it; and where we would have remained all night if an obliging farmer with a Farmall tractor had not noticed us and pulled us out.

Mallards and Slim Bean's Slough

There were four in our party staying with the Browns as guests, not boarders. The other wife, Mrs. Johnson, had brought no gun, she was still at the audience stage. So there were but three guns to be examined and discussed, before retiring for the night. They were removed from their cases, put together by both Bill and his son Carl, held up to their shoulders, aimed toward the heater or a picture hanging on the wall.

"She sure is a fine feeling gun!" appraised Carl rubbing one hand along the stock of a twenty-guage double barrel.

"Not the 'killingest' gun," said J—, "but lighter and more fun to shoot."

When four o'clock came the windows of the little house were still squares of black ink. Not even the stars lightened the darkness of a morning that was still night. It was cold, too. Dressing became but a series of quick jerks into heavy woolens, trousers, socks and high rubber boots.

We sat down to an inviting breakfast. The Browns had been awake for hours, it would seem. Mrs. Brown had cooked for us. Susan, pretty, seventeen years old, would wait on us.

"She's the last for us to educate," said Bill as the slender girl put down before us steaming cups of hot coffee, generous slabs of hot toast covered with country butter, fried eggs with bacon, and a generous platter of buckwheat cakes. "She's our baby." In the next room, already assembling our guns and shells, Carl waited for us to hurry. "My other daughters is all married and gettin' 'long purty fairly. We've always given 'em the best of everythin' and tryin' to make 'nough now so's Susan can finish. Education, I tell Mrs. Brown, is a good thing these days when no tellin' what a girl might have to do next. But times is a little hard with us—when you figger on bills for operations on my eye—." Bill had a cataract over his left eye.

Susan smiled. She was happy. She had returned from school in another town where she did chores to pay for her board, in order to assist her mother.

At five o'clock, accompanied by Bill and Carl, we were sent off with a paper bag generously filled with sandwiches, cookies, fruit, and hot coffee in thermos bottles. No guests in a very grand house were ever treated better.

White frost covered the road. From a black night, the forbidding hoary world round us became touched with a delicate flush of pink, the first break of day. Dawn rose over the sleeping fields with their rows of Indian corn rising in the shape of wigwams, and mounds of shocked hay blanketed by Jack Frost's handiwork.

We were bound for Slim Bean's slough and

nearly there. After we had parked the car we walked—a mile—over a raised platform of wooden planks just wide enough for two feet, no railing. Thus we reached our blinds in the trees and the brush, on the edge of a wide pond. Overhead a grey November sky of early morning. The wind rippled the open water ahead of us where the wood decoys, already set out, bobbed on the waves. From somewhere near came the splashing and flapping of live decoys in a pen, while from a greater distance we heard a mechanical duck-call. Hunters were already stationed in their blinds. The Johnsons had gone with Carl to a stand further down the pond. There was something freshly gratifying about the feel of the early morning wind in our faces.

"That big bunch o' birds've gone!" exclaimed Bill with a grunt, when his one good eye quickly discerned that not a single wild duck remained on their resting place of the previous night. "Some o' these duck-hounds, 'bout these here parts don't know daylight whan they see it." He cleaned off the end of his call on his leather sleeve as he spoke: "If Slim don't pay no more 'tention to th' fellas he lets th' rest of this pawnd out to, I'll tell him he can keep—not only one—but both his blinds tomorrow. . . . 'Tain't worth even *two* dollars with that big bunch all shot into. . . . I

always did say that thar' three ways of doin'
things. A right way, a wrong way, and a way
that'll do." He pushed the end of the call into
his mouth, tried it out, loudly, and withdrew it.
The tame mallard-decoys heard the call and commenced their symphony. "I'm kind'a thinkin'
Slim cheats on baiting them thar pens, anyhow!
I told Carl to get Ramrod's place but somehow
some rich fella from Ottawa's leased it for th'
season. . . . He ain't no kind of a shot no how
his pusher told Carl. Can't figger why a fella
that's no kind of a shot has to lease up th' best
grounds on th' River so's no other body gets a
decent place. . . . Why if I'd a had th' money
thirty forty years ago I'd own not one of these
here pawnds but the best damn duck shooting
lands on all the River. It's a crime the way prices
've gone up! . . ."

Four mallard drakes soared by, from over the
trees behind us. We ducked our heads. They had
not only heard Bill's voice but spied us still mon-
keying with our guns, and stowing away the paper
package that would attract any wild duck's wary
eye. "Quack-quack"—came a hopeful chorus of
welcome from the mallards in the pen. But of
no avail. The wild fowl were gone. A minute
later a few sprigs sailed high over our heads, and
woodeys whistled by, close, serenely confident—

the season on them being closed—of their own assured safety.

Bill was right. The main body of ducks that always fed there were gone. And, besides, the wind was not favorable for our particular blind. But as yet we were not cold, and there was a board on which to sit, patiently. One duck came in, circled, came back, cocked its head to one side and peered at the tame birds quacking below, disapproved of them, flew on; we could see it circle back of the trees near the blind in which were stationed the rest of our party. Bang! And another shot. We heard the splash when its body fell. Once more all was quiet on the pond.

A second later, from an unseen blind in the distance, rang out an unearthly yell—combination of a Swiss yodel and an Indian warwhoop. It echoed for miles, growing stronger in sound as the echo appeared to follow the horizon like a boomerang.

"Some fool calling geese!" boomed old Bill from the clump of trees behind our blind where he had stationed himself on solid ground. "He'll scare every duck in a thousand miles with that call of his'n."

"Snow-geese," announced John as we both peered upward to see high in the sky, four separate flocks flying in exquisite formation. The sun, attempting to penetrate here and there between wind clouds, had discovered the birds. It shone now on their white, black-tipped wings, and made them glisten. One flock were Canadian geese, greyer and not as beautiful. Their honkings drifted down to us far below like the tolling of tiny bells. Majestically, in perfect squadron formation, onward they flew, bound for southern fields.

But wait—this was no time to admire far-away geese! Bill was wrong. The call had not scared any ducks, for at that very moment innumerable flocks of mallards seemed to come in from every direction at once. The sky was black with their silent wings—for they too, like the geese, were high over the trees.

"Don't move a muscle! . . . They'll see you. . . ." The man beside me whispered. Forty or fifty more birds now appeared from behind us, headed in the direction of the large mass passing high above. These new arrivals were close enough for us to hear the *cheep cheep* that comes from their wings, and not their bills as I had at first believed. But John made not the slightest move.

"We can't shoot into as large a flock as that," he explained in a whisper. "But get ready now while those lower ones turn. Get your gun ready —then *don't move!*"

In the meantime Bill had tuned-up on his duck-call. The tame decoys in a nearby pen heard, and answered. The air was bursting with the cries of barnyard mallards now adding their notes to Bill's mechanical mouth piece.

Twenty or thirty wild birds turned, circled round the trees behind us, but instead of dropping lower, they appeared to be rising.

"One or two will come back—you watch!" John said.

Almost as he spoke, four mallards separated themselves from the rest. They commenced a second circle, this time lower.—Their wings beat hard and close. We could hear them, distinctly. A breathless moment!—

They swung in, close.

"Now give it to them!"

John, a true sportsman, waited for his partner to shoot first.

She lifted the gun. Before getting it into proper place, the cheek not down close enough, she pulled the trigger. The shot rang out.

No bird even slowed its flight. Instead, upward they soared, alarmed.

Bang. . . . Bang.

A duck—the exact one she had aimed at—dropped its wings and made a nose-dive into the pond.

John laughed. "Well, why didn't you shoot

the second time?" he parried. . . . "I didn't mean to wipe your eye like that, but I couldn't wait any longer.

"Shush! . . . Here come two more. Now *get* one!"

The two he mentioned—a pair of green-winged teal—had arrived unexpectedly. They, like the mallards, had been intrigued by our bouncing wooden blocks. They commenced a circle—disappeared behind the trees.

"Get ready!" came another whisper.

And from behind, a violent, throbbing, irresistible quacking from Bill.

The birds now came back, almost ready to drop into our decoys.

"Quick!—"

We both shot—Two birds fell.

What a moment!—My first duck lay, turned over on its back, drifting on the crest of the current.

"This is a peach of a gun!" I managed to say, swallowing hard. "I like it much better than that fancy double-barrel of yours."

It was a twenty-gauge Remington pump, thirty-inch full choke barrel. Easy to handle, well balanced. John had given it to me a short time before, figuring, I believe, that having to pump in between each shell I might be more accurate than if I felt a second shot could follow immediately. Some men, I have since discovered, consider pump guns as dreadful things—unsporty, not stylish, and so forth. Five shells would perhaps be unsportsmanlike if the companion shooting alongside you had but two. I used only three shells and this did not seem all out of proportion for a gunner who would probably take a week to get one day's limit. Besides, for a woman experiencing her first season of duck shooting my gun was inexpensive, and pleasant to use because of its lightness; also there was no second trigger to confuse the finger.

Although now and then our shooting during the early morning, noon and forepart of the afternoon proved fairly exciting, and even the beginner managed to bring down another bird or two— there followed long dull stretches in between when we became conscious of our cold feet and cold hands, cold ears and noses. The sky dulled and the surroundings began to assume bleak and dreary aspects of grey water, frowning sky, and bare trees.

Bill Brown had become bored with his lonely stand behind in the trees. He waded back to us. "Say! . . ." He exploded as he stepped into our blind. "Tomorrow mornin' we'll be out 't daylight before'n them pot-hunters. And we'll go somewhare else, too! A fella would starve t' death if he depends on his meat from this here pawnd. . . . I only heard your friend shoot half a dozen times all day!"

Bill was disgusted. His feelings were written on his face plainer than writing.

But good duck day, or poor duck day, there was a fascination about the sport hard to describe. Since then I have decided it can in a way be likened to the charm of trout-fishing, a sport so utterly dissimilar; but comparable as to its æsthetics, one might say. For the charm of the more gentle pursuit of trout-fishing, the suspense that keeps you casting hour after hour, day after day, is the never-failing hope that "some day you will catch a *big* one." While with duck shooting the suspense is not, size: instead—the faint and never-dying hope that some day you will fire fifteen shots and strike the fast-flying and elusive target fifteen times.

Also, the whistling of wings as the wild fowl soared by; the persistent call of the penned decoys; the added duck persuasion of Bill; the mystery of the fall sky; the day as it progressed from the glamor of pink dawn to early morning; noon and a "snack" washed down by a cup of hot coffee; late afternoon and a large evening flight with birds lighting all about us; all, all these events contributed to make that first taste of shooting ducks something long to be remembered.

One more day we spent with the Browns. Bill,

the first evening, had bewailed all during supper the absence of "th' big bunch o' birds!"—he had expected to find on the "pawnd," and which, through no oversight of his, had not materialized. Sunday's blind, as Bill hoped, did decidedly better for us all. Before noon the two men had bagged their limit. And Bill hoped our trip had been more worth while.

While we carried our luggage, muddy boots and sundry belongings from his house to the car, Bill's voice followed us about. "Th' black jack ought'a be in next week-end," he was saying. "If you folks care t' come back—just send me a wire!"

We thanked him. We were anxious to be off, so as not to necessitate motoring too many hours in the darkness of night.

"Say!" It was Bill again. He continued to stand by the car, loathe to let us depart. . . . "If you or any o' your friends would ever care t' lease up any good land on th' River somewhare, I can still bait them pens." His good eye broke into a smile, and he cleared his throat. The sun played across his thick glasses, and illumined for us, as though they were two small round picture frames, the gentle, humble soul behind those two eyes which had already witnessed the yearly migrations of thousands of wild ducks.

"I'd kind'a enjoy one more winter with th' birds," he said.

III

"Big Bunch o' Birds"

OLD BILL HAD HIS WISH. The next time we saw
him he stood beside a pen of English call ducks.
The wiring of the pen he himself had staked out
on four posts; the birds' wings he had clipped;
the pen he had baited with corn from the barns
of a farmer whose unemployed land we had managed to lease. Up to his waist in the muddy black
water, clad in hip boots and blue overalls, he was
talking to those flapping, preening creatures as
though they were human.

"That old hen thar is as tempe'mental as a
movie queen," he called to us over his shoulder
as we paddled up to him in a canoe. "She man-
ages to flop out o' that thar bunch o' wire two
three times a day. I tell her she's foolish. I
have t' come along and toss her back every
time."

Bill had also, with the part-time aid of Carl,
and George and others of his tall grown sons,
built four blinds, two on either shore of the over-
flow-lake which opened into the Illinois River.
These, he planned, would provide stands for four
guns, or two at least:—in case the direction of the

wind happened to be unfavorable for one side, the other shore might be used.

Each Friday evening when we reached the primitive little camp, just north of Chilicothe, Bill, anticipating our arrival, would have made a blazing fire in the stove of the cook tent, and a fire in the stove of our small sleeping tent close by. He himself would be cleaned up and tidy after a long day working with decoys, shelling corn, carrying it with the aid of a duckboat to four pens of hungry decoys, and lastly sweeping out the floor of the two tents. He would be seated in the cock tent, contentedly smoking his pipe, reliving in his memory his earlier days on Illinois marshes, and comparing his feelings, then, perhaps, with the feel of a duck-blind at dawn now when he was getting old and four sons were growing up to take his place.

The camp was crude to say the least. Our few acres included a swampy terrain between the main line of a railroad and the body of water that emptied into the river beyond. Two tents with board floors, and a shack where Bill slept and where we kept extra cots in case of visiting hunters, was all that it could boast. Tramps, or hoboes, often passed us by, and saw our gasoline lamps giving off bright fitful glows, and smelled our steaks broiling and onions sizzling in the pan. Squirrels from gnarled bare overhanging trees gave a nightly series of highland flings on top the canvas tents; and owls hooted eerily from hidden nooks.

The greatest joy of camp-life was the fact that there was no one to bother us, nothing near but the woods and waters and wild life thereon. And we could indulge in a never-to-be-forgotten childish desire to mess about with dishes and frying pans and cooking of food.

When it rained we were nearly washed away. When the thermometer registered freezing we had difficulties in keeping warm. The pathway leading through the woods to our boats was a lane of black oozy mud, in places deep and boggy, so it necessitated at all times waist-high rubber boots.

I say the camp was crude, and we were all but washed away when it rained. But it was luxury, it was safe, it was always dry, compared to another camp on the bare wind-swept shores of an Alaskan bay.

As for the cold, are there many places in the world colder than a duck-blind on a raw November or December day when the skies are bursting with snow and the north wind whistles through you? I doubt it. I hazard even the Arctic because mukluks are cozy and warm, and feet in wet rubber boots for hours at a time are like icy appendages. In a duck-blind your nose feels as though it belonged to someone else, and your frost-bitten hands you rather wish were not part of the same person who a short while before stood by a warm fire, waiting for the morning coffee to boil.

I remember one morning particularly. Early as usual. There were three guests, men, since we had no accommodations fit for any other kind of visitor. They were not minding the rime that spread over tents and dead grass and mud. Instead, they were terribly anxious to be off. "A wonderful duck day!" was the consensus of opinion as we dried the last plate and the last spoon and tucked them neatly into their proper niches.

Needless to say, these three guests were assigned to the two best blinds, John going off with one. Bill and I were offered a new and admittedly experimental location, nearer camp and back in the trees. Rather hard for old Bill to be relegated to me, and the worst blind, while Carl and George accompanied the real hunters! But he smiled and bore it well, said we would do "better'n th' rest of 'em."

We settled down into our blind, our feet in rubber boots standing in icy mud. The sky was grey with great wind clouds scurrying by.

"Ducks'll sure fly today!" Bill grunted as he peered upward and around, scanning the horizon with the same pleased appraisal as a drama critic employs when he studies the opening scene of a play and feels he is about to witness a fine production.

Ducks did fly. Flocks of them, yet seldom by our blind. Bill called, and called, his mouth fairly exploding with the wind and extra tempting blows on the important object he squeezed between two hands. Now and then he managed to coax a few mallards to notice our blocks and harken to his tempting calls, but they never came in close. I wanted desperately to get several. The most encouraging sight of all was the heartening sight of many enormous new flights which were obviously still in the process of travelling. High in the air, they had not yet lighted. Certainly they would never notice us—in our poor blind. "Thar'll sure to be a big bunch before'n mornin'," Bill hazarded as we stood there, heads just rising above the brush, two pairs of eyes peering at the wild fowl soaring by.

"Quick, stoop down!" suddenly ordered Bill. "Comin' in low. Take your time. Wait until he gets closer."

One mallard sailed in, alone. Bill, I could feel, was tense and stiff as a statue. Now came his enticing call.

The bird, being alone, was extremely cautious. He looked over our blind as though to say, "I didn't see that pile of stuff there yesterday." Then he scrutinized again the bouncing wooden decoys. He was still too far for shot gun range.

"What th' hell's th' matter with th' old hen?" whispered Bill, referring to his favorite English call duck in the pen nearest our blind. "She hasn't squawked for an hour." He tried again his own loud imitation, adding the long throbbing note at the end.

The wild bird became interested. The last throbbing appeal had worked. He swung in nearer the string of alluring decoys.

Bang. . . . I did not touch him. He darted upward. Bang. . . . This time—he folded his wings.

"He sure turned over on his back!" chuckled Bill excitedly. "He'll never wiggle again. . . ." A second later—"Here's 'nother! . . . Shoot!" Again a bit of luck. Now we had two ducks.

There were long periods, though, when nothing happened. And while we stood there, or sat there, listening to a steady bombardment from two other blinds, Bill tried to appear unconscious of the situation. He relieved his pent-up emotions by divulging gory tales of outlaw years on "Th' River." Market-hunting, poor sportsmanship, murders!

Eleven-thirty came. My feet felt completely

frozen. But I had had, for me, still further luck, two more ducks.

Bill commenced to grow increasingly restless and inquisitive concerning those other blinds from whence came shots, and to where seemed to head all the mallards. No longer could he control his bubbling—but tactfully withheld—curiosity.

"Guess I'll kind'a shove down thare 'n see how th' boys are doin'," he finally unburdened himself. "We've got all th' cheese sandwiches 'n I remember Mr. Borden likes cheese. . . . I told Missus Brown that he does."

The sandwiches in his pocket, off he went, headed through the dark woods, splashing in and out of pools of deep and muddy water.

More ducks in the air. More shots from the other blinds.

"Say!" his voice sputtered, echoing through the trees, as he returned not long after, not able to wait to speak until he could reach me, "Them fellas 've already got their limits! A hunter's sure got no chance in this here hole." When he had waded back to the blind, and stepped in, he added, "We'll wait until they've picked up and then sneak over there."

More hours of being frozen? The heavens would surely pour out its white burden at any minute! . . . But I could not let Bill down.

"Big Bunch o' Birds"

"Let's have a little hot coffee, Bill?" I agreed, "And then—we'll decide."

The sportsmen, in the two duckboats, pushed by us a short while later and waved gaily. "How are you getting along?" called John. And I knew what he was thinking. He displayed a fairly guilty grin.

"You might as well be in Slim Bean's slough on a butterfly-day as to sit here," Bill answered for me. "But we've sure seen th' birds goin' in to you fellas."

The six men, drifting by, laughed and pushed on.

The instant they were out of sight we made preparations to move. And in the second blind we remained until mid-afternoon. Bill had drawn the Missus as his charge; she *must* do well.

When at last we trudged homeward, cold and hungry and tired, over the muddy path leading to camp, the snow had begun to fall like a white curtain trying to blot out trees and sky. Bill carried the bag. There were, needless to say, not fifteen birds, but enough to satisfy me, and to make Bill feel as though his day had not been all in vain.

"I always did tell Missus Brown it ain't so bad for a woman t' shoot," he was saying. "She kind'a keeps better track o' th' old man when ducks are flyin'." The last he added with a wink of his good eye.

The final week-end of the season came. Bill was anxious to have it the best of all. He had, from the beginning, been handicapped by our not having leased the land earlier in the season, and as a result the pens had not been baited as early as they should have been. Therefore we could not expect as large a number of wild fowl resting and feeding on our lake as we hoped, and as Bill would have liked.

"I seen mighty close t' two hund'rd mallards drop int' that thar second pen this evenin' whan I'd finished throwin' in the corn; and I saw many mor'n that'n th' first pen," Bill could hardly wait to inform us as we jumped out of the car. "Thar'll be a world of 'em a layin' out thar on th' lake— right now. If you folks care about a walk down thar in the dark you'll hear 'em splashing for miles on every side."

That evening, our next to last in camp, we sat long in the snug cook tent, discussing not only mallards, canvas back, widgeon and teal, but Bering Sea, schooners, whales and Brown Bear. Bill had gone to Alaska on John's boat thirteen years before. The December night whistled now against the tied down tent flaps and swooped away over the prairies to the south and east. When supper was over Bill took out his pipe, lighted it, and began to talk of a muskrat with whom he had that week come in daily contact. Before he finished, his big voice booming pleasantly as he helped us clear the table and put it in readiness for a four-thirty breakfast, we one and all began to feel that this muskrat's acceptance of the world was not only an industrious one but his perseverance something that many of us could emulate—and profit by—when hard times come. That little fur-bearing friend of Bill's—whose most recent labor had been washed away for the third time by rising waters—with its undaunted persistence and energy, had completely won the old man's heart. He had applied to it his own philosophy of life. "He just won't give up," Bill explained. "He comes back—and starts all over I don't know how many times. That's what I tell Missus Brown and Susan—a fella should never know when he's down and can't get up. . . ."

The next morning when the last flapjack had been turned in the pan, and the last cup of coffee enjoyed, we were ready, guns on our shoulders, rubber boots pulled up, warm jackets buttoned close round our necks, to push off in the frosty darkness preceding dawn for our boats and distant blinds. As we plodded across the lane of frozen mud a host of black birds fluttered out of the treetops above us, chattering in loud and fearful unison.

Bill led the way. He was nervous, it seemed. Had not he told us, on our arrival the evening before, that "A big bunch o' birds've come in" . . . and "Thar'll sure be a world of 'em—"?

A cold grey dawn crept out of the east as we settled ourselves, noiselessly as possible, into the two duckboats. Now, the opposite shore stood out, a black line, in the whitening streak of day-break. We were two parties. Bill and I in one boat, bound for a nearby blind, John and a friend in the other. They were to take the farthest blind, on beyond.

Silently we pushed out of the inlet between the tall bare trees. Bill and I led the way for the rippling boat in our wake.

We reached open water. Day rose, higher. In the queer distorted light we strained our eyes looking down the lake.

At that instant came a deafening whirr. Hundreds of wings beating at one time; hundreds of birds rising from somewhere behind us. Then, out from the edge of the dark woods they came, flying towards us, passing gracefully over our heads.

Bill stood motionless, push-paddle stilled.

"From the pen!" he whispered thickly.

He waited, hoping for—something more.

"Big Bunch o' Birds"

We did not move. Nor did those in our rear.

Then the something did happen. Something thrilling. Something for which Bill had worked—and anticipated—during two whole months.

Off the lake rose the most enormous number of wild fowl I had ever dreamed of seeing. Multitudes of dark bodies flung themselves upward, blackening the sky of early morning, rending the stillness of the air with their disturbed cries.

Bill said not a word. But he resumed his quiet pushing.

As we skimmed forward, headed towards a concealed blind in the brush along shore, thousands upon thousands of birds continued to flutter up from the water ahead.

IV

PART I

Ruffed Grouse with Duke and Jake

"Good mornin'," Ben Allen greeted us with a smile, as we drove up to a cabin in the north Michigan woods. He had been standing on the porch and, when catching sight of our motor, had hastened down the steps to give us welcome.

"What luck . . . this fall?" John called out.

Ben had not heard. "Got here in good time, didn't ye?" . . . he continued. "A bit before I was expectin'."

We had as yet not been introduced to the other members of the small hunting and fishing club situated a few miles north of Grayling, which we had joined recently because of its reputation for good partridge shooting as well as trout fishing. Nevertheless, we were curious concerning their success in the field since the opening of the short season on ruffed grouse three days before.

"How about birds?" John persisted. "Or has it been too warm?"

Ben was helping us unload the car.

"Purty good," he replied, pursing his lips, and

40

turning the question over in his mind. This was his club, he worked for it all year round and he loved it. "I guess ye might say a good many," added he with some hesitation. "But the birds seem to be gittin' up so awful wild this year. My goodness they're wild! . . . They'll hardly lay to a dog at all. . . . Why it warn't so long ago that a fella might git a few shots—'stead of just watching 'em scare up a mile ahead of ye."

Ben, whose entire life had been spent in the open, summers on a trout stream, winters hunting and trapping, possessed the clear penetrating eyes of a woodsman and the tanned leathery skin of a man accustomed to constant exposure of sun and wind and rain.

"The other crowd 've all gone off—early. I told 'em I'd wait here fer you folks, and Mrs. Richards will have lunch ready soon," he explained as we lifted the last gun, the last box of shells and the last suitcase from the back seat.

We made for the cabin, dragging in all the paraphernalia for a week-end in the autumn woods. As Ben opened the screen door, out bounded Duke and Jake, a pair of English setters that had been given us recently by a friend. They had arrived here by express. Originally they had hailed from *Glenwild*, had been puppies in our kennel, and we flattered ourselves they might remember us. Duke, small and slender and more black than white, reached us with a rush, but Jake was heavier and his body, you might say, a trifle underslung. The preceding winter he had met with an unfortunate accident: on his way to Florida an expressman in the baggage car had managed to drop a trunk on him. Jake's hunting for that season had been over. "When Jake gets tired he sometimes limps a little," his former master had told us, when he gave us the dogs. "But I can't give him any hunting at all where we live—and old Jake is good for a few years—anyway."

Eagerly the two black and white dogs rubbed against us, sniffing our clothes, our guns, and never ceasing the happy wagging of curly tails. Duke, after fully scrutinizing his new master with his greenish yellow eyes, laid back his head and barked, pleading for him to make haste. While Jake, his nose twitching with an inward emotion, trotted importantly back and forth along the porch, personally conducting each armful of luggage that we were now bearing into the main room of the log house where a warm fire blazed on the hearth.

George Pirtle, a geologist by profession, and an associate of John's, reached the club soon afterward in his own small car. He was to be our guest, and a possible grouse meant much to

George, for he, like ourselves, had looked forward to this Saturday and Sunday for many months. Discovering oil in some one else's well would never be as thrilling to George—he had already admitted—as discovering that he himself could bring down the trickiest of all upland game birds.

As for me, though it had been explained with emphasis that this sort of gunning takes infinitely more skill and patience than duck shooting—I, too, entertained hopes of some success. Had not those birds of the Saskatchewan prairies looked as large as barn doors? . . . At any rate, bird or no bird, I had, like the pioneer wife of old, climbed upon the seat of the covered wagon, and must take the consequences. And *he* had said: "I'd like to see you get a partridge." He really meant it, too.

A half hour later our party set off. Duke and Jake, loping ahead, eagerly led the way back to the distant and higher hillsides in their October radiance, the hillsides of yellow and copper and gold.

"Them popples up there is the place," Ben pointed to a covert probably two miles away. "Ye purty near always find pâtridge in a fine clump of popples like that." He pronounced the *a* in partridge like some Bostonians are prone to pronounce it in Harvard and car. Yet he was far from being a product of that effete city.

Towards those distant popples we headed. John carried a Wesley Richards, sixteen-gauge double-barrel gun right-barrel cylinder and left-barrel modified choke, thirty-inch barrel. He prefers sixteen-guage for grouse, and any good shell with seven and a half shot; perhaps using number six late in the season if birds are wild. Mine was an L. C. Smith twenty-gauge double-barrel which had perhaps too much drop for field shooting—its second set of barrels being good for duck. If a single-barrel gun is used for these birds, the hunter in our family thinks it should be modified choke. If double-barrel he likes right barrel improved cylinder and left barrel modified. But all sportsmen have their own ideas on guns and shells and very few seem to agree entirely.

In our firing line of four—we had suggested to Ben that he bring his gun—we were careful to keep in a straight line as we climbed up and over rough ridges, threading our way between trees. We descended again from every hill into hollows out of which it became equally difficult to climb. We tramped to right and left, pulling our legs in and out of thick undergrowth. Half of the time I was wondering what to do with both feet—if a grouse should start up suddenly; and the rest of the time I spent in shoving twigs and branches away from my face and trying to hold the gun pointed skyward, safety on, ready to be hastily raised to the shoulder, slipping off the safety with the one quick movement. A split-second loss of time would be certain to be a miss.

"I'd sure like to clamp down on one of these babies!" George was saying as he tripped over the fallen stump of a tree and righted himself.

"Fine grouse country!" John exclaimed as he topped a ridge and gave a sweeping glance at miles of wooded country in its finest autumn raiment, stopping to watch for a moment whether the dogs had turned and whether I was keeping up. Duke was working but a few yards ahead. Jake was far away.

The air, redolent of woods and berries and leaves, was fortunately cool and bracing. And the hunt itself—the search and the suspense—was all part of the thrill. Far away could be seen the bluish-grey smoke from a small camp fire. It twirled upward into the afternoon sky like delicate floating feathers. While at our feet, in patches here and there, waved a crimson weed whose tufts ruffled in the gusts of wind like stubbles of red wheat. The out of doors, in all its flaming colors, was a veritable artists' paradise, more like a canvas in some gallery where a visitor might stand before it and comment incredulously: "Nature *couldn't* be like that."

Jake in the meantime, wandering too far afield, was tiring himself needlessly. He had had no hunting in over two years and perhaps, having been a puppy in the southland, imagined he was again following the haunts of quail. He had been employing just the opposite tactics from what we needed. A dog who hunted too wide might easily scare up one of these wily birds long before the guns came into range. Duke, on the other hand, though he too had had little experience afield during the preceding two years, was behaving quite as a grouse dog should. . . . Few grouse dogs would ever win a place in a Championship Field Trial. . . . Seldom was Duke more than twenty yards ahead of the advancing line of guns. Eyes alert, head up, stern down, and nimble feet moving cautiously—stylish Duke seemed to have understood at once the sort of situation he had been put down to meet. Conscientiously he quartered every foot of ground within our radius. First right, then crossing in front of us, swinging back to our left he went, leaping like a hare up and over tangled clumps of underbrush. After each blow of the whistle he would turn simultaneously, look round towards his master and handler, and obey the instructions given by a wave of the hand.

John held the center of the line; his wife, the

right flank. "Well . . . walk up!" he suddenly ordered me. "Novices must never lag in the shooting field, you know." A second later, "Not so fast! Can't you see, you've gone ahead of the line?"

Ben, from the left, cocked his head and grinned at me, sympathetically. Being the universal male he was undoubtedly wondering why a woman in the shooting field, under any circumstances?

Whirr . . . heavy wings beating by, behind us.

"What was that?"

"A bird . . . *dammit!*" some one muttered. And John added: "I probably scared it up—talking to you. . . ."

Duke had heard the bird. He stopped and wheeled abruptly. Ears tuned, he turned his head and asked the hunters from where the bird had risen.

"Where'd it go?"

"Over there, I guess—in that thicket. Got up behind us," Ben deplored, casting a longing look in the general direction the wings might have gone. "I didn't see it. . . . Did ye?"

Nor had anyone else. So there was no use going after it.

"Jake! . . . Come down. . . . What do you mean? . . . Come here, sir," his master called, sternly, but not unkindly. "Come here—I said."

Foolish Jake, in his ever-widening casts had undoubtedly flushed the game, so I was saved any further blame. And now Jake had proceeded to race after the bird, as fast as his short legs could go.

"Too bad . . . in this open place, too! We won't get many shots as easy as that one," Ben lamented feelingly. For we had reached an opening in the thick woods.

"Jake doesn't seem to know what it is all about," his new master apologized. "We'd better leave him home tomorrow." Jake's doom was sealed but Jake was still oblivious of the fact. He pranced up to us, a trifle sheepishly, smiled, and wagged his old tail. "Careful, Jake . . . steady now." The dog wagged his tail the harder, and tried with his dark pleading eyes to explain his mistake. Then he walked away, dropping his tail.

On we went, heading now towards an even denser patch of woods than any we had heretofor attacked. We reached a barbed wire fence and started over it.

"Always break your gun—before climbing a fence!" Jake's master now scolded me. "Most accidents occur when climbing through fences. Well, why pick that way? You're sure to be behind a tree if a bird gets up. That's the trouble with all beginners. You always wonder why trees are in the way."

Ruffed Grouse with Duke and Jake

The fence accomplished we reloaded our guns and once more progressed on our way. Every second—the suspense had quickened since hearing the sudden rush of wings behind us—we expected to flush another bird. In the thick woods where we now were the odds would certainly rest with the game.

At that moment we heard a dog's pleading cries. It was Jake and we had forgotten him. His right fore leg caught in the barbed wire fence, white curls tangled round the barb, while trying to extricate himself he had only made matters worse. When we released him he was all but human with his thanks and gratitude. He had scratched his paw and from then on he limped, stopping now and then to lick the injured member. Poor old fellow, he was not being in the least useful and all at once he seemed to sense it. From then on, tail down, he ceased trying and stayed close by our heels.

Not very similar was this search for the ruffed grouse in its natural surroundings, to the shoots of raised game in England and on Long Island, on preserves where beaters drive hundreds of birds into the air at once. Nevertheless, driven birds do take the utmost skill in marksmanship but no energy or labor or knowledge of the hunting country and habits of game which constitute, after all, much of the sport of gunning for birds on the wing. The two types of bird shooting can not be compared for we were in a sparsely settled section of the United States where wild creatures still abounded. Hunters and dogs were being out-played by a gallant feathered creature whose favorite ruse is to permit a hunter to pass, while it crouches unseen; then suddenly to laugh at him by leaping out from behind his back.

Our hunt indeed was hard and earnest. Nor was it similar to shooting on Long Island during the latter part of the eighteenth century. Here is an excerpt from a sketch published in 1783, "Heath-hen shooting on Long Island." After describing the bird and giving directions for finding it, the author goes on to add:—"I should here avoid at-tempting to describe the several articles of con-veniency, such as horses, *chairs*, provisions, *liquors*" (my italics), etc., "necessary for this di-version.—Suppose my party to consist of two gen-tlemen. I would provide a single horsechair" (whatever that constituted?), "a servant in the sec-ond chair, to carry the dogs, provisions, liquors, tea, sugar, etc., and spare powder and shot."

Now, in comparison, I contribute my own field notes hastily scribbled just prior to Jake's acci-dent, while I sat down for a moment of rest. . . . "In the meantime we have pulled legs through dense growth rising to knees, and first up hill, circle, climb, climb, then down, then back up. Over fallen trees, in and out of holes we go. Can hardly navigate any further in heavy boots and long underwear and two heavy socks. From knees down not as tired, but halfway to the thigh the ligaments seem to pop in and out of sockets. How do the dogs do it? For every yard we tramp Duke covers a hundred on his short legs. I guess I'm soft, all right! Better get in shape before trying it again. The tension of possible game any minute keeps me moving. . . ." Since that week-end, my eye-opener on the subject of upland shooting, I have been glad to read: "No other game bird puts the gunner to a harder physical test than does the grouse . . ." so wrote the distinguished Colonel H. P. Sheldon.

Not long after Jake's accident we reached a likely spot where birds should be found towards evening.

Whirr!

Another partridge got up wild this time ahead of Duke. Off it catapulted a mile a minute. Despite its swift speed it steered its way between a labyrinth of trees.

George raised his gun, let go, aiming at the swiftly vanishing form. The shot cracked out, loud in the still autumn woods. The rest of us waited, breathlessly. Yellow leaves fluttered off two trees. But no bird dropped.

"Missed it!" . . . he bewailed, with a soft curse under his breath. "Why didn't any one else take a shot?"

Duke, disappointed, and still wondering whether perhaps the bird had fallen after all, glanced back at the man who had shot, and then, seeing he had been correct in his first surmising, started slowly ahead, disgusted. It was obvious by the way he drooped his tail, like a black plume between his legs.

The two other hunters had been out of range. It had been George's bird.

So on we went. The sun was dropping in the sky. It was colder, too.

Duke was at last making game. We were to have a fair chance, a fair warning. His neck had stiffened; he had lengthened out his lean body and straightened his tail. Nose aquiver, he stole towards the scent, cautiously, not yet certain. . . . When zzzz—again the thunderous take-off of a partridge's abrupt rise from the ground and its wings fast making speed: a breath-taking, startling sound like nothing else in the world. Each time —only the one bird. No doubles, no bevies.

Ben and John pulled their triggers, instantaneously. The bird darted behind a tree. John had taken a half-snap-shot. Two shots had pierced the stillness, now a third. The quarry, fast reaching a particularly dense growth of trees, suddenly, when the last shot resounded, shot straight upward, towered high in the air . . . fluttered uncertainly. Then it folded its wings and came down —as though a magnet had pulled it out of the sky.

"Hit it plumb in the head!" Ben shouted excitedly and then laughed aloud. "I missed . . . aimed too fur to the left, I guess."

Duke scurried to the spot from where the sound of the falling bird had reached him. He found it, carried it back with the utmost tenderness, his happy eyes shining as he laid it, not a feather ruffled, at the feet of the man who had brought it down. His master leaned over and picked up the dead partridge. Then he patted the slender black setter and said, "Good dog, Duke." The little animal cleaned his mouth off with his tongue, retasting the freshly killed game, and shivered with a sudden and overwhelming sense of importance. While Jake hovered near, tail suspended between his legs watching his brace mate being petted and, as well, the bird that his new master grasped so carefully in his left hand. "Pretty bird, isn't it, Jake?" his master now addressed the unfortunate dog whose mute black eyes still inquired why he today had been so unsuccessful.

I recalled an illustration in colour of a Ruffed Grouse, strutting. A magnificent half-circle of fan tail almost as gorgeous as the full regalia of a peacock, and a wide ruching of white and brown feathers forming a thick stand-out collar round his neck. The picture had made me compare his spring beauty with the paintings of vain Queen Bess when armored by her finest robes of Court.

So beautiful and yet so clever this wild bird! It did not seem that any one quail or duck or prairie chicken or snipe or woodcock could ever give the same satisfaction and supreme combination of both splendor and sport which this feathered beauty had offered. It is quite true that in the length of time we had stalked this bird—for it was stalking as much as though we were stalking big game,—we would have bagged several quail. And quail are not considered, not often anyway, easy prey. And what epicures these grouse are! "Patridge eat mostly winter-green berries and wild grapes. They eat very partic'lar like," Ben Allen had told me. No *gourmet* of the nineteenth century chose with more discretion.

"Well, we ain't skunked, anyway!" now exclaimed Ben, as once more we started forth, the heart put back into us by a degree of success.

The afternoon was wearing on. Four o'clock and one bird. Though it must be taken into consideration that we did not start off until after luncheon,—had only been out some two hours.

Despite our hard work only two more grouse did we see that evening. The first rose, wild, far ahead of us when the crackling of dry underbrush announced the approach of an enemy, and the denseness of trees hid its escape. The second called forth quick snap shooting on the part of John and Ben. And as they both shot they shared the spoils.

The sun dropped out of the sky and disappeared beyond a flat ridge, a red ball no redder than the scarlet maples edging the low skyline like plumes of fire. The odor of winter-green came more strongly than before. The tang of earth and leaves and trunks of trees, as a white mist rolled over the land and night came down, was as strong as the tang of an open sea.

The four fellow club members had returned ahead of us. Sounds of splashing and voices ensued from the bathroom. Their two white setter bitches lay stretched full length in front of the blazing fire, too weary even to give attention or curiosity to Duke and Jake, our setters that had joined them and were themselves asleep before we had even rubbed off our guns.

At dinner, when both parties sat at one long table, we compared our hunts. Over the hot chicken broth we learned that they in an all-day hunt had bagged four birds and a rabbit. Yet they considered themselves good shots. This "partridge-hunting" then was never any easy matter.

"Are you coming back here for the trout fishing?" the man on my left was asking. When I nodded he assured me that the stream offered "Fine fishing!" Then John across the table explained to me: "You're talking to Mr. Peet, the world's champion fly-caster."

The eldest man of the party was deaf. He had, though, caught in some miraculous fashion the words *trout fishing*. His hand was at his ear. "Don't believe a word my friend tells you, Mrs. Borden," he said. "Don't forget that once a fisherman—always a liar!"

He drew a loud laugh from the oddly assorted gathering. Greedily we now fell upon the next course offered to us, heaping platters of fried chicken, fresh tomatoes, celery, mashed potatoes with glorious country gravy, banana cream pie, and black coffee in large cups, filling our grateful and empty stomachs. Discussion of grouse and grouse-dogs soon became neatly stirred in a strange brew composed of the proper flies for the opening of trout season six months later; and whether a good grouse dog should sneak towards his quarry, or, instead, come to a sudden halt.

Jake Redeems Himself

Our four canine companions enjoyed as avidly as we had, their own heaping platefuls. They were given, not alone scraps, but juicy bones of fresh beef. Back they trotted happily to the fire and more sleep. So did we. And early to bed.

George said, after he had wished us good night, "I'll sure clamp down on one of them babies to-morrow—or know the reason why."

*   *   *   *

PART II

Jake Redeems Himself

THE RABBIT HOUND bayed as the sun rose. Bed had been the coldest spot in the world. One person, at least, dared not stir an inch on the clammy cotton sheets, despite two heavy army blankets, thick wool pajamas and socks. When the hound bayed she raised her head off the pillow high enough to witness a heavy frost, glittering like crystals strewn across the tops of the two cars which had perforce, for lack of any shed, stood outside all night. And the piles of men's clothing with other signs of hurried dressing still remaining before the hearth on her arrival at the club the morning before, flashed across her awakening

57

consciousness. There was something to be said for it—dressing before blazing logs!

This morning the six men, chatting loudly, and laughing at what they said, dressed before the fire while her teeth chattered alone in a damp little room with thin walls like paper.

The dogs were already outside, anxious to be off. Jake limped as he attempted to gallop towards each person who came out on his way to breakfast, whirling his tail up and down and around, a bit like a white feather duster.

"Jake's pretty soft. We'd better leave him home," John said as we patted him, and walked on to the cook cabin where hot coffee waited.

Anticipating a long hard day, eight hours afield, we managed to make away with most of the generous menu which Mrs. Richards set before us: Grapefruit, cereal, eggs and bacon, toast, pancakes, doughnuts and even a plate of cookies.

Before starting off we tied a reluctant Jake to the flag pole by the side of the main cabin. While we fastened the chain, he sat back on his haunches and watched us, shivering, his curly body fat and round, and then laid back his head and howled. . . . "The begginest dog. . . ." the Mississippi stable boy surely would have said of him that morning. Then, once more with the philosophical manner of the day before, he ceased his howling and stood upright on three good legs to follow us with his eyes while we stowed guns and extra sweaters into the car. Duke, self-conscious and pleased with himself, approached his brace mate of the preceding day to look him over once more before he himself would be off with the guns and men. It was then that Jake managed to wag his tail, in as much as though he said: "You've got to do the work for the two of us, this time, old friend."

The day that followed proved more what we had hoped, and our territory better hunting ground. Soon after going afield the men got two birds. The birds, though, were still singles. When they flushed wild, or Duke pointed them, it remained anybody's guess as to the direction they would take. Each time the thunderous take-off! Each time the tremendous and unbelievable speed! How to pull up the gun, cover the swiftly vanishing form darting between trees, and pull the trigger all in the flash of a second? To me it seemed nothing short of a miracle. Sometimes too far distant; again straight away and low; or a spiral, or catapulting straight towards you, all but sweeping off your hat with their fast-beating wings. And those still cannier creatures who waited unbudgingly, hidden until we had passed, and then zzz—up they rose, were most provoking of all. Admiration for anyone who could nail one of those birds was a real admiration.

The high light of the day took place when we put up a bevy of three. Duke had pointed a partridge that lay not more than six inches from his nose. The three men shot, bringing it down like a lump of lead. "I can't claim it!" George muttered truthfully as he reached down into his pocket for more shells. The other two laughed, and took their time in reloading for we had begun to believe all birds would be singles. . . . One more feathered bomb zoomed up out of the deep grass. *Bang*. . . . *Bang*. . . . Someone had let go but the swiftly hurtling bird was already out of range and disappeared behind a forest of limbs. And again —this time we were warned by a suspicious rustling of leaves—the startling rush of a bird's wings! The game flushed directly in front and a few yards ahead of me.

Ben and George took a chance shot and missed —they both, they claimed, having waited on me. John's barrels, he having taken a long shot at the second bird, were empty. He was, moreover, at the far end of our line.

"Why didn't *you* shoot?" he called out, addressing me in no uncertain terms. "That last one was your bird. You'll never in all your life get a better partridge-shot than that!"

Jake Redeems Himself

Then he laughed. To the guide he added: "My wife was paralyzed, I guess. . . . Lucky you and Mr. Pirtle didn't wait any longer." Nevertheless, they had waited too politely to get the bird.

By afternoon I was completely done in. The men announced their intention to make a wide circle—on foot, of course, the car being parked miles away—and when satisfied, return to where we stood. So I thanked them and declined to go along, gladly lying down in the deep grass. In a few moments I sat up and jotted in the notes—: "By lunch could scarcely lift the legs and hadn't pulled the trigger. J—'s handsomely carved gun is much too good for me. All except the carving is wasted. It's this way—When the dog points I'm supposed to hurry up alongside but I'm usually much too tired to hurry—as well as breathless. J— says all beginners are like that when the dog points. He calls it creeping paralysis! Besides. . . . I never see any bird soon enough to shoot! When I fell down this morning *he* called to find out whether I had any mud in my gun? Mud in my gun? . . . I felt like saying I wished it were in his eye! . . . My legs simply won't propel me one step farther and my feet weigh a ton. I hear three shots. Hurray! What luck? Wish to goodness I were there. But

I'm wondering how I can even make the three-mile grade of bumpy uneven up and down ridges —into holes and over tree stumps—back to the car? I certainly wish George could get a bird! I'll always be cheering for the underdog in the shooting field after today. Personally, I've ceased to expect a partridge."

Duke came leaping like a hare out of a nearby thicket. How on earth did he get there? Almost simultaneously I saw a bird. It looked enormous as it sailed low over briers not far away.

This was my chance. I knew it. The notes were quickly shoved aside, two shells pushed into empty chambers. Sneak it while the men were not looking! It was my bird! . . . Before I could even reach the alleged spot where I had marked it down—back the three men came, laughing to themselves as they emerged from the same thicket as the dog. They had, miserable beings, spied the person who had been left behind, now break into a run. They remembered the condition in which they had left her. They knew full well that no one as exhausted as she had looked, could possibly get up and run without good reason. So on they hastened. Before she realized it, the three men were beside her, and they were again marching in that beastly line of four.

The dog pointed. They moved up—closer. The

grouse, my grouse—rose two hunters away. . . . John's shot, and his shell struck home.

I knew, when they followed me, I would never forgive them! And I felt more certain that I would never forgive them when I discovered that the three shots I had heard while resting, had already given them two more birds.

By this time Duke was slowing up. We decided he had had enough hunting for one day. If we had had a fresh dog in the car we would never have permitted him to work so hard and so long at a stretch. But he was the wiry kind of a bird dog who will seldom admit to being tired.

We had seen approximately a dozen birds and were bringing back but six. Yet we felt we had accomplished something, in taking these, considering that all four guns were not up to their work. Although the bag, and not the individual score was of primary importance, it still mattered that George ought not to return without himself bringing down a partridge.

When we reached camp, stepped out of the car, and walked up to Jake, still tied, he was beside himself with joy at seeing us. Once more he sat back on his haunches and raised a curly white paw, pleading for release.

"Would you like to give him one more chance?"

John suggested as we all patted Jake. "We could try along the edge of the stream. . . . Might be pretty good there—late."

A tired Duke in the meantime had managed to propel his weary legs as far as the stream, where we could see him drinking, then he stretched out on the grass.

So off we tramped—this time Jake accompanying four hunters—towards the stream, where the birds would also be coming to drink.

Jake had learned his lesson. He not only had cured his sore foot, but this evening, displaying a surprising understanding as to what was expected of a grouse dog, he never reached out further in his hunting than a few yards ahead of the guns. When we had no luck and several minutes went by, we decided to spread out in an even wider line, cover more territory. George, with Jake not far from his side, climbed up and over a low hill and disappeared.

Darkness was closing in on us.

In another few moments we heard a shot. We stopped. Listened for the second shell. But no. Just the one.

Down over the hill they trotted, man and dog. And a more pleased, grinning pair—a person could seldom see. George carried, clutched safely in the right hand, his bird. Jake hugged close to the man's long legs, beating his tail back and forth against his high boots.

"You should have seen Jake!"—George shouted. "He not only pointed it—but retrieved it . . . without my saying a word."

When one member of the party reached her room to do the necessary packing she found the two four-legged comrades of the hunting-field— stretched out on the bed fast asleep. Jake heard her and opened his eyes. He shook his curly body, and wriggled comfortably against the soft pillow.

"Haven't I deserved this soft spot as well as Duke?" his contented eyes implored. While she, on her part, wondered whether Duke and Jake had discussed together, before falling asleep, the horrible truth that their mistress had brought down nothing?

Only poor consolation came, when crawling into bed hours later, she murmured to herself: "But he did say he was afraid I couldn't get a Ruffed Grouse. He didn't really expect me to." A duck blind with hundreds of birds in the air at once, many shots instead of one, and a place on which to sit when tired had been a sport more suited to my humble skill.

SPRING

V

Lure of the "Salvelinus Fontinalis"
IN THE EYES OF A FLY FISHERMAN'S WIFE

"The kind of man to go fishing with
Is not the man who has fame or goods.
A title's nothing, and wealth's a myth,
When men are up in the great green woods.
It's not the man who is deeply wise,
It isn't even the polished man—
But one who is handy fixing flies
And turning fish in a frying pan."
DOUGLAS MALLOCH.

THESE FEW LINES were the third stanza of a poem that hung on the walls of a log cabin in the north woods, the same log cabin where we had stayed during the grouse season. As we read it, we saw outside a peaceful forest of white pine and birch, and the red of the setting sun reflecting across a quiet stream. We remembered the doe with her fawn who had wandered down to the water's edge to drink; and the partridge dusting in the road, who rose, at our approach, and fluttered away.

We smelled again the trout frying in the pan, and thought of our long day in the stream. We were tired, pleasantly so. Round us sat other fishermen. As we stood there waiting for the remainder of our party to come in, we realized that we had never seen any of these people before. Yet a quiet feeling of friendship and well-being had stolen over us all. We were all interested in the one and same thing. Nothing else mattered. "A title's nothing, and wealth's a myth, when men are up in the great green woods."

Although this was the fourth successive Saturday at the same place, doing the same thing, we were, nevertheless, looking forward to many more similar week-ends.

What then is the lure of fishing for brook trout? What constitutes the charm that sends young men and old men back and back again to the same stream to try and catch the same fish? Why this excitement and bother concerning a catch that often measures but seven or eight inches? "Inches?" I used to say to myself, let us talk in pounds. Trout-fishermen, it would surely seem, are as mad as March Hares.

Yes, so they seemed to me—once upon a time. It was quite absurd, all this futile chatter of flies and reels and rods—and here again inches and ounces instead of feet and pounds!—absolutely ridiculous. They were quite mad, all fly fishermen!

Then I decided I had solved it. It was the season of the year. The season of the year that finds most men light in the head, all lovers impatient, and trout fishermen with a special impatience that nothing can cure but a fifteen-inch trout. . . . Spring! . . . How I once dreaded the arrival of the first of May. For the Head of the House not only contracted a bad case of spring fever, but became at the same time unbearable in the family circle. We—even the children were forced to admire his selection of flies and taught to know their names—had to hear constantly about flies—flies—flies. We walked, ate, talked, and slept with visions of flies. The maid, who attempted in vain to keep his hunting and fishing clothes tolerably clean, and a little bit impervious to moths, once spent three days and nights in search of a battered, scuffed-about, felt hat "with flies on it." Being French, she searched nervously every shelf, careful to inquire of no one as to the missing article, the whereabouts of which she evidently should have known, and muttering under her breath: *"Un chapeau avec des mouches. Un chapeau beige pour aller à la pêche."*

Poor soul, she has returned to France carrying with her a mental picture—a nightmare—of a cedar chest heaped with the sorriest belongings *she* had ever imagined could possibly belong to such a *Monsieur, un homme du monde.* Laundries, dry cleaners, tailors, she had suggested, a hundred times. *"Mais non . . ."* with a disgusted shrug of her gentle shoulders. *"Le Monsieur dit-non!"*

How surprised she would be to learn that *Madame* now has as precious and sorry looking an outfit as *Monsieur*. For after having angled for rainbow in Glacier Park, for steelhead in the Rogue, for cutthroats near Lake Louise and for Dolly Vardons and grayling in Alaska I have at last succumbed to the lure of that most exquisite little game fish, the brook trout.

In the first place, a trout stream is the cleanest, cheeriest, most exhilarating thing in nature; and the most obliviously peaceful. The instant you step off into the cool refreshing depths which carry the bubbling exuberance of sparkling wine, and the shimmering water rises about your rubber-covered legs to your knees or waist, you feel your blood tingling to your very finger tips. Wading such waters is bound to instill even within the heart of a confirmed urbanite an ecstasy of feeling that cannot be painted in words. It is an emotion that sings within you a nameless melody; a melody of sheer and simple beauty composed of the airy chirping of birds; the sun's brightest rays breaking against you; the clumps of waxy yellow marigolds that grace the line of shore themselves like spots of sunlight; and the sky above, the stream below. Last, but not least, in the same way that a camp brings back dormant desires of childhood to hide away and play with dishes and the cooking of your own meals; so fishing a stream appeases another childhood pleasure— *wading*.

Oh, the peace of it! Wine that slips smoothly down inside you. Wine that makes you forget anything, everything except the day, the hour, the moment, and a fiendish—again puerile—desire to catch a fish.

Thus now, as spring comes round again, and the guns are stowed safely in their cases, and the first of May hovers deliciously on the horizon of our plans, there are two of us who circle round the house—anxiously peering into chests and drawers in order to assure ourselves of the condition of last year's waders, old soft hats, fishing jackets, creels, and nets; also the necessary tackle boxes holding fly oil bottles, leader boxes, line greasers, aluminum fly boxes, mosquito dope, reels and gadgets of every kind, variety, and importance, to say nothing of the precious rods lying side by side, begging to be released from their long winter's nap.

This is no treatise on how to fish—that is, on how to hook a large brook trout and many of them; since the writer of these chapters is still unable to present a Royal Coachman or Queen of the Waters with any degree of skill. In fact each time a more profound discouragement, on the subject of the right wrist, sets in. Furthermore, when trying to describe the joys of angling there is, as the deaf one so ably expressed it, the danger of finding yourself "once a fisherman—always a liar!"

"It's so beautiful—I don't really care whether I ever land a trout!" Helen, a fishing companion of ours expressed herself, as she and I started bravely upstream one May morning. It was the second or third time that either of us had angled for brook trout, and the first time upstream with a dry fly. This, as every fly-fisherman knows, is mightily different from downstream fishing with wet-fly. As she cast, trying to reach out to the dark mysterious pools lying ahead of her under overhanging branches along the shore, or the faster riffles swirling at the base of fallen trees, she took notice of the green banks where wild cherries and dogwood were in bloom; and caught the fragrance of violets in winter-green and young spring grass drifting out to us there where we pushed against the current, wading up the center of the glittering stream, the big Manistee River in the northern part of the lower peninsular of Michigan.

But it was not many minutes before she was throwing out her line with all the zeal and art she could muster. Of course she wished to coax a trout on to her lure—and soon! I think it was not long before she began to forget the surroundings—they became a part of her—as she cast with more and more feverish desire for success.

When suddenly her line—ahead of her in the stream—tightened with a sudden tug, and the light rod tipped the water. She snapped it with her wrist. A battle waged beneath the surface of the rippling stream, for *fontinalis* is an underwater fighter. It started to run with the line. The fisherwoman gave it more line. Again even the longer line became taut and the lively fish suddenly zigzagged across the water.

"Don't give it any slack, whatever you do!" shouted Andy, her husband, who had appeared unexpectedly on the high bank above us and was watching the performance. "It's a good one!" he shouted. "Keep your rod up."

The fish and line now started coming at us downstream. The slack was becoming more difficult to control. She tried to reel in, with no success. The fish came faster. When it reached abreast of the person who held the rod, the wary creature straightened out and darted towards a rotting log that lay close to shore.

"Watch out—or he'll get under that snag!" further instructed the voice from the bank. Husbands, at these moments are horrible nuisances like backseat drivers. If they cannot assist, why must they yell?

We stood close together, the smooth current swirling about us. Somehow I felt that her quarry was half mine. I could all but feel its game fight on the end of my own line and the wide circle of the rod as it trembled in her hand. I thrilled with each frantic swish and renewed demonstration of strength beneath the water. Therefore, I was equally worried over this recent development of the snag.

There followed an ominous silence—a sort of darkness before dawn sensation. Neither of us could figure out what would follow but hoped the next step would be an advance for our side. Then my friend began to draw in her line, steadily, dropping the extra yards of it in the water with her left hand. I was proud of her. She was handling a difficult situation in a professional manner. The struggling fish, at the end of her leader, appeared larger in size than he had looked at a distance. He was a brook trout worthy of anyone's catch. He, too, seemed to realize a professional hand was attacking his diminishing hope for liberty. He was tiring of the battle.

Lure of the "Salvelinus Fontinalis"

We had but one landing net between us. It hung over my left shoulder.

Her line, with the prize on the end of it, was coming in nicely. The trout was fairly close to us, now. The next problem would have been solved easily if she could have but slung him, line and all, up on to the shore. This was impossible. To have attempted it would have resulted in a lost fish and probably a broken rod.

Something had to be done and soon. So I grabbed the net from off my shoulder and dropped it down into the mirror-like water. The pretty fish, plainly exhausted, was swimming, hook in its mouth, towards it. Then came a neat swoop with the net.

But we were wrong. It was not exhausted. All it needed was a sight of that white string object looming on its horizon. With a tremendous swish of its lovely body, a swish that tore the hook from its mouth, our prize was gone.

Now her husband had the opportunity of his life. Loud laughter peeled out from the nearby hillside. When the first outburst of merriment had died down, he called out: "Don't either of you know enough to approach a trout from the rear?"

Again laughter that shook way down into our nerves.

So that proved an early experience of how not to try and net one of these game little fish. Lessons like the last mentioned one come often when valiantly attempting to learn this baffling—and often comic—art. Coördination of your wrist and arm counts for a good deal; and of course—using your own so-called common sense in competition with a sporty living creature.

There seem, however, to be still other elements that loom large and prevent many spectacular achievements, other hindrances that detain the fly fisherman from taking limit catches:—whether it has rained recently or is about to rain, the temperature of the water as well as the air, from where the wind is blowing, and finally the art itself of matching his lures to the hatch on the stream each time he fishes. This last knowledge appears to be the *ultima thule*. And now that we as a family have amassed quite a worthwhile collection—that is, as far as looks go—of artificial flies purchased at various times and places, we are to have still others tied each week, prior to departing for the woods, in order to match whatever hatch might be due. The little pamphlet issued, that apprizes fishermen of the dates of hatches, has become an important part of our already complicated equipment.

*   *   *   *

Lure of the "Salvelinus Fontinalis"

Although a true fly fisherman would never deign to enter into a serious argument as to whether bait or flies actually catch more trout, there can be considerable said on both sides of the much hashed-over question.

One Saturday in the latter part of May with four in our party, we started off for a certain stream, this time the Pine. We were enjoying the drumming of woodpeckers, the chorus of frogs and the clear liquid notes of song birds. Again we experienced—as every one does when wading a stream—the exhilaration and peace that held us: the beauty and freshness of spring, the melody of nameless rhythm that crept deep within us. In the company of our guide two of us were heading for our favorite pool, a deep dark one under an overhanging willow. But—when reaching there, to our disappointment we found two other fishermen already firmly established.

"Bait fishermen!" exclaimed the guide scornfully. "Plunk a lot o' bait down in them holes—and a fly fisherman ain't got *no* chance."

Sunday, a week later, as we rested on the banks of the Ontanagon, eating our lunch, and now and then glancing up at a blue sky shining between branches of trees white like chalk, we were discussing the annoying habits of trout when we noticed a large fat person wallowing upstream making quite a noise. He saw us, there on the bank, and stopped to talk. We compared luck and flies—as all fly fishermen seemed to do. The upshot of our encounter proved that the fat fisherman's luck had been better than ours. So he generously informed us of a wonderful pool and swift riffle downstream, "where the two tall Christmas trees are." We thanked him, and explained that three fishermen were already there.

"Oh," said he. "*Them* guys is *bait* fishermen! I kin stand right 'long side any of 'em—and catch all kinds o' fish. . . . Bait can't hurt no water." He spoke with an air of finality.

And here is an episode that took place at the little club on the Manistee.

At the long breakfast table covered in a bright red and white checked cloth, there had been much lively conversation concerning flies—dry, wet, wing, or hair—their separate merits and which ones we should try that very day. Two elderly members—one the deaf one—knew all about the stream, the best holes, the correct flies, and had apparently been enjoying of late considerable success. So we listened to them. They had decided the Cahill would be "just the ticket."

That day, after valiantly plodding both up and down stream, changing flies, falling in once and getting wet up to the neck, several times hooking on to trees and snags, acquiring an aching wrist and back, and tired legs, but only five trout—not very large ones—I started back towards camp, proud of a small catch. It was eight o'clock. Bullfrogs had already commenced their husky evening song which sounded not unlike riveting in a great city, and dusk was slowly drifting across the river. Then I spied smoke curling out of the chimney of the cook cabin, a welcome promise of supper.

The two elderly fishermen had reached the Club. They stood near the steps of the main house, hoping some one would come along to admire two limit catches of large trout. . . . The joy always has to be taken out of life! My five little brook trout suddenly seemed like five dried-up minnows lying in the creel, covered with a handful of green grass.

Late that same night, while trying to fall asleep in a dampish bed after imbibing two large cups of coffee, a man's voice came wafting through the open window, floating over from the bachelor's wing in which the two elderly fishermen of the limit catches had their rooms. He was talking with his friend and being deaf his voice was always pitched rather high. I could not help but overhear.

"Say!" he said, and stopped to clear his throat.

"I think we had much better luck today with worms than we had yesterday with minnows— don't you?"

Another subject that comes in for its share of strong opinions is the subject of fly rods.

Everyone is entitled to his or her own ideas, in the same way one hunter prefers a certain make of rifle, and another disagrees heartily; or one sportsman swears by an over-and-under, while another considers it not only an acquired taste—like caviar—but an affected one, also thinking that in fast work you are too apt to cant the barrels in cross fire. So it is with rods, opinions are equally divergent.

The fly fisherman whom I know the best happens to prefer for all-round wet nd dry-fly combination a five-ounce rod, eight-and-a-half feet long. Though, for dry-fly fishing only he likes a four, or a four-and-a-half ounce eight-foot rod. We have, for some time past, given and exchanged rods and guns on birthdays and Christmas so there are now several makes represented in our leather case; Leonards, a Thomas, and a four-ounce Granger which is one of mine, and comparatively inexpensive, perhaps considered in the same classification as the maligned pump gun. With it I use a very light reel—incidentally also inexpensive—to balance. After several hours of casting, the lighter equipment proves far easier on the arm and wrist.

But why all this interest involved in the makes and weights of stylish rods? Why can't we use just a plain *pole?*

I thought this when one June evening, seated at an attractive dinner table and enjoying a bounteous meal after eight long hours in a stream (in the upper peninsula of Michigan near Waters Meet), our host related a story of stories—and a true one.

Rochester, as tireless a fly fisherman as some one else I knew, still chortled over the memory as he tried to tell us. For it was a grand joke on us all.

Both he and John had been casting from a raft far out into the depths of a pond where big trout were known to lie. Side by side they had been careful not to disturb their own, or the other's chance, of catching a large trout by stirring up too much water and making too much splash. There they had stayed for quite some time and had caught several—not small ones—but not large enough ones, either!

Along came a boy in a flat-bottomed boat, a boy of about twenty who was wielding a hugely long yellow pole—the kind used by fishermen for lake perch. It had all the ear-marks of a perch-rod except it lacked the bobbing cork. With no reel, and using worms, he commenced whisking his bait out into the same pool in which the two men were casting.

For some time he continued to throw his line into the wide pool but caught nothing, did not even have a strike. The men of our party, on the other hand, were pulling in ten, eleven, and twelve "inchers" at fairly frequent intervals.

Finally they felt sorry for the lad and called over to him that they would fix him up with a fly and leader.

The boy, with the heart of a true fisherman, cheerily called back, "Don't mind catchin' nothin'. I'm just out for sport!"

Nevertheless, continuing with no better luck he soon accepted gladly both fly and leader and once more settled back into his flat-bottomed tub to try his luck. In fact, by this time his boat was alongside the raft and he was still oblivious of the fact that he might spoil the other fishermen's water. Whereupon he returned to the business of whipping out his line.

The men waited and watched. There was no use trying, they decided, until the "kid" moved away.

After one or two awkward and noisy swishes that heaved his line and leader and fly plunk into the water with a loud splash that could have been heard by a trout for miles around—an expert fly fisherman has written somewhere that a noise like this would sound under the water like an avalanche or a cannonshell—the boy hooked a sixteen-inch brook and plopped it into his boat with a wide proud flourish.

How would any expert fly-fisherman explain this one?

SUMMER

VI

Hunting the Great Brown Bear

"Alaska" had long been a magic word in the family household. Even the children knew that Daddy had been there twice, had shot bears, had been shipwrecked, had brought back and kept in his room a collection of delicately wrought Indian and Aleut baskets and bottles, and ivory carved by Eskimos. He possessed, too, a large harpoon which had something to do with whales, and hundreds of snapshots of storms at sea, of men on the deck of a ship, or on land, whose faces badly needed shaving and resembled Robinson Crusoe.

It must be thrilling—Alaska! I, too, caught the mysterious glamor that the children sensed. A country where hunter, gold miner, trapper, scientist, or explorer apparently encounters any number of hardships and tribulations, yet also a territory which most men hope to visit at some time, and to where, when once home and surrounded again by the comforts of civilization, they can scarcely wait to return.

As time went on, and a vacation of several months seemed possible, the question before the house became:—where should we go? Alaska was suggested. It was quite obvious that for one of us the hankering to return *once more* had become irresistible, so the question was resolved in favor of—not Europe or Egypt, or Africa—but Alaska. For the North has a lure that when once given into, becomes in the blood a craving that is almost a disease like a craving for liquor or dope.

Out came maps and charts by the score. Could I stick existence on a small boat for such a length of time—a good many months. Did I mind getting sea-sick? Then, with a finger on the globe pointing horridly close to the North Pole, "We'll hunt walrus and polar bears up there in the ice-pack. I'd like also to get to Wrangel Island. Only half a dozen ships have ever been there. . . . You'd be the first white woman." And then, with a grin, "Do you still think you can make it?" . . . Make it? I knew it would be either a case of making it, or the summer would be spent alone, taking care of home and children.

So nearly every afternoon and evening during the following winter we were kept busy preparing lists of clothes, guns, ammunition, food, and camping outfits for the long and hazardous voyage. Sunday afternoons we spent on a rifle-range, teaching me how to shoot.

Happily, there were friends to whom the unusual trip appealed as much as it did to us. There were to be seven of us, three men and four women.

Two of the number were to go no further North than Nome, while the rest of us were gayly preparing to spend July and August in the Arctic ice. And now, five years later, I, too, hanker to return *once more* to Alaska, *once more* to the great Arctic ice-fields under the glare of the midnight sun.

*   *   *   *

When writing of grouse in the uplands of Michigan, of canvas back in Saskatchewan, of Illinois duck marches, or even of trout streams, there needed little explanation. They could be imagined fairly clearly by the reader, if not already seen for himself. But Alaska is different. "We've been to Alaska," is as confusing and all-embracing a statement as though you might overhear a man in London declare that he is—"On his way to America."

For the immense Territory of Alaska covers an area greater than the whole of France, Germany, and the British Isles. It comprises three distinct geographical divisions: Southeastern, Southwestern, and Alaska proper. The first includes the far-famed scenery of the Inside Passage, with the thriving towns of Juneau and Ketchikan. The

91

second; the long expanse of land reaching from Seward to the far western tip of the Aleutian Islands, embraces also the Alaskan Peninsula, Kodiak and the Pribiloff Islands, while the main body of this sprawling possession of Uncle Sam extends thousands of miles to the North up into the Arctic Ocean.

Should you, then, not be able to voyage further than the termination of the inland waterway, you would have seen great natural beauty but really would not know the territory any more than you would know the United States if you visited only New England. . . .

Now, I will get on with my story.

On the twenty-fourth of May our two-masted schooner, *The Northern Light*, neared the Alaska Peninsula. Our long-anticipated hunt for the Great Brown Bear would soon be realized. We were completing the crossing of the Gulf of Alaska and a miserable crossing it had been. Five endless sea-sick days! Five nerve-wracking days and nights when many of us wondered how we could ever go on; how we could even attempt the voyage of many hundred miles further north. The Pacific had been rough enough—despite its name. This gulf of Alaska—unbelievable! And what would the Arctic be like? . . . We began to wish for a dirigible—anything but a ship that must ride the waves.

At last, through port holes opening on to the deck above we, who were weakly reclining below, heard: "Land Ho!" No time did we lose in climbing the companionway to view the more than welcome sight of Land.

Gone were spruce-tufted islands, and virgin forests, gone the magnificent Fairweather Range; here we saw gaunt bare islands with sheer dark cliffs jutting out of a rolling blue sea. The arid though cactus-flowered hills of Arizona would have seemed like fertile gardens in comparison with these islands edging the coast of Southwestern Alaska. While off to starboard the Alaska Peninsula heaved its jagged bulk, a fringe of volcanic mountains etched against the skyline to the height of some ten thousand feet above the sea.

Gone also would be the Indians. The natives of this country would be Aleuts.

Not a tree, not a shrub, did we see, and we were greeted by the cries of thousands of waterfowl, as we dropped anchor in a peaceful harbor off the settlement of Unga. It was here that we were to take on board our necessary guides and with them proceed to a location they were to have selected in order that we might procure specimens of *Ursus*

gyas for the Field Museum of Natural History.
. . . The names of Alaska bears are puzzling to
all but scientists. The large Brown Bear of the
Alaska Peninsula is,—thanks to the information
given me by Dr. Wilfred H. Osgood, curator of
zoölogy at the Field Museum,—*Ursus gyas:* gyas
in Greek, signifying, appropriately, giant. And
the vernacular for this bear being Peninsula Brown
Bear. Whereas, in many cases you will hear
hunters term every large brown bear of Alaska,
"The Kodiak Bear," which is confined to Kodiak
Island and is, in a strict sense, *Ursus midden-
dorffi.* Whether they are of different species or
only varieties of subspecies, Dr. Osgood claims is
not so important as the fact that there is really
some difference between them.

Unga, where the guides awaited our arrival, had
its uneventful birth after the discovery of a near-by
gold mine which had since played out. It boasted
of some two hundred and fifty souls, seven whites
and the rest Aleuts. In this little place lived
Nekita and Pete and two of the packers; while
a few miles away, at King Cove, a good deal
smaller community which sprang up round a
salmon cannery, dwelled Robert and Albert and
Mike and a third packer: packers seemed to be
mythical beings who were to remain in camp and
hold themselves in instant readiness to march out

and bring home a dead bear. Now I cannot even recall their names. They were there to be bossed by the guides, and do most anything and everything.

A rivalry, we soon realized, existed between the two factions: a rivalry that continued in an increasingly heated manner when we later divided into two hunting parties in our hard search for the bears that were destined to make a group in the Museum case.

We remained one night anchored off the town of Unga, attending a dance given in honor of the birthday of Pete's twin sons. The following morning when our whistle blew three times, our goodby to Unga, thousands of gulls, Kittiwakes mostly, fluttered close to the two tall masts, and escorted us on our way. Horned and tufted puffins flopped lamely across the waves, while cormorants, murres, and guillemots joined the multitude of gulls in their excited celebration of our departure. Even two whales flashed their huge glistening bodies, flicked their death-dealing flukes, spouted, and then, of a sudden, decided to sound.

The *Northern Light* reached Pavlof Bay, her destination for this first leg of a far longer journey, on May the twenty-sixth. The surf in the bay, running too high for a boat to be sent ashore, delayed the guides in their hope of making camp on that first afternoon. And while we stood on deck, busily sorting and weighing the large stock of provisions which we must take with us for our intended stay of four weeks, a bleak and desolate land crashed our imagined expectations of glamorous Alaska. We would be existing there on that flat wind-swept beach protected from the northerly gales by no more than a low treeless cliff, and looked down upon by two snow-capped volcanoes. Yet Pavloff, the taller of the twin peaks, was so utterly beautiful, so majestic in its conical white serenity dominating the dreary landscape, that we forgot the prospect of bleakness and the inconveniences of winds and waves which were detaining us in our eagerness to row ashore and commence the hunt.

"You'll see four thousand walrus to one brown bear!" the sixty-year-old whaling-skipper exclaimed with emphasis, and a laugh, when he approached and assisted our plying open of one crate. Cheery news! We had hoped to procure a whole group, male, a female, and two three-year-old cubs. Then I fell to thinking of Bill Brown and the little tent on the Illinois River. How he had expatiated on the hardships and the glories of "Kodiak Bear huntin'!" How he had turned over on his tongue the retasting of the evening "when he had follered an old beggar for 'bout ten miles afore he could pull th' trigger," and delightedly embellished his story by relating all the difficulties of finally packing the heavy skin and skull to camp many miles distant. The weeks of incredibly difficult hunting, and success at last had added magic to his still vivid memories of an Alaska he had not visited in eighteen years.

As for John, he and the two other husbands had smiled, knowing and annoying smiles, when they at last decided that the four women of the expedition might hunt for bear. He and Rochester, big-game hunter as well as trout fisherman, had tried the sport before and knew what, in such country, the verb *to hunt* would constitute.

Glancing once more over the desolate beach and tundra while we continued to count and arrange cans and boxes, we four began to realize that we might have bargained for more than we could possibly carry out. I recalled, with a new interest, the many wintry afternoons suffered on an army rifle-range, learning, learning, learning. In every position they tried me: upright which they called "off hand shooting," the sitting position, and finally flat on the tummy. Also, from every distance. In fact I could almost feel again the bruised and aching shoulder from firing off my Springfield seventy-five times in fairly quick succession. And I recalled, too, the gentler form of rifle practice indulged in for the past six months within the privacy of my bedroom when with an air gun I aimed for five minutes each morning, and five minutes each evening, at a series of postage stamps stuck against the chinese-figured wall-paper. I thought again of the *chic* French maid who had had so much trouble with the family hunting and fishing clothes, their exasperating un-tidyness, their evident shabbiness, and her brave struggle to retrieve *Le chapeau beige avec des mouches*. For she was, many a morning and eve-ning, completely amazed, and at a loss to under-stand what had happened to *Madame* when the telephone buzzed and buzzed and her mistress continued to point a silly little gun at a row of pink two-cent stamps.

"Come up on your target, no jerking or you will have to find it all over again," had been the explicit directions. "Fire—when you see the sight just on the target." And, oh the literature on ballistics, and bores, and trajectory, and velocity! Like digesting an unpalatable food. Though an unpalatable food might keep you awake with in-digestion the studying of ballistics and trajectory can be guaranteed to cure insomnia.

Peering across the choppy water in the direction of a barren wasteland I mused as well on the pleas-ures of a comfortable home, on my love for three small children; I appreciated the remembered services of kindly and faithful domestics, and the longed-for taste of a rare beef steak and fresh asparagus. Here we lay at anchor in a bleak Alaskan bay, preparing to set forth towards a shore where winds and rain would make us their helpless playthings, and our six small tents would be the only signs of human habitation. Even the *Northern Light* would leave us, would be, upon our departure in the launch, piloted to Canoe Bay, a safer berth fifteen miles away.

During the evening we sat in the main cabin, listening to hair-raising tales by the guides of this man and that man who had been attacked either by a wounded bear, or a she-bear with cubs. It was then we were instructed never to leave camp without carrying a rifle.

On the second day, though the sea continued rough, a load of tents and crates, and men, were at last dispatched ashore. The temperature was about forty-two and a cold penetrating wind blew from the southeast. Two trips were made and soon from the decks those of us who remained on board could watch the tents being staked out and lashed down with ropes.

Camp would soon be waiting for us with our supply of hams, bacons, corned beef and corned beef hash, beef stew in cans, canned fruits, vegetables, and potatoes; cans of butter, dried eggs, evaporated milk, soups, plenty of jams, marmalades, cookies, milk chocolate, and raisins. A selection which would not tempt an epicure, certainly, yet food that would keep us going. We had added to it, while being delayed, a hundred pounds of freshly caught cod and flounders. The flounders were delicious and made what the French chef on board the schooner called: *Sole à la Alaska.* Codfish cheeks proved a good enough dish for any one.

As for clothes! Nothing more than we wore on our backs and could tuck under sleeping bags. Tent floors under the cots would be too damp— the guides warned we would probably get rain every day—to be counted on as extra space. After much planning we reached a unanimous conclusion on the necessity of an extra pair of trousers, two flannel shirts, several pairs of woolen socks of various weights, high rubber boots, and other lighter boots with rubber feet and leather tops which turned out to be most preferred of all foot-gear for this difficult going, two pairs of heavy wool underwear, a hunting jacket, a felt hat that would shield the eyes and shed a light rain; and last, but most important of all, a light-weight rain coat, one that had hood and coat all in one piece which would keep the rain from dripping down our necks, and a pair of light oil skin trousers. Next came the choice of drugs, the most important being, we soon discovered, a good foot cream to relieve exhausted feet each night after the long hunt.

At six thirty in the morning of the twenty-eighth we climbed down into the launch, surrounded by duffle bags, rifles, kodaks, and fishing tackle. I mention the date because it was important. The hunting season closed June twentieth and each day was precious.

In order to approach our tents, after once landing on the beach, we must cross a pond that lay in a deep hollow of sand. Not having on rubber boots there remained only one way of making it— and that by the ancient means of "pig-a-back." I can see us now with our belongings strewn in heaps, safe from the white breakers, while ourselves were being transported in this absurd manner to the opposite side.

Near a clear-running mountain stream the men had erected camp. It constituted a main tent where we were to cook and gather in the evenings, our four smaller tents, a large one for the guides and packers whom we had taken on board at Unga, and another for the camp cook and cookee.

At sunset came the rain of which the guides

had warned. Also for four days the wind blew from the wrong direction to make it useless for us to hunt the particular territory within reach of camp. One of the familiar annoyances encountered in hunting big game! . . . So there was little to do for all that time but occupy ourselves in other ways and wait as patiently as possible.

In order to assure themselves of better hunting the men, with their respective guides, took turns in a second or temporary camp which they established ten miles away, near a location termed by the guides, *The Glory Hole*. We, left behind, did the necessary mending and washing, helped the cook, talked, read, fished for Dolly Vardon trout, studied bird life, watched the activities of red foxes, took dozens of still pictures and hundreds of feet of movies, pressed the wild flowers that dotted the tundra like dabs of color from a brush, wrote in our diaries, and tried a half-hour of target practice, daily. Besides, we attempted to tramp—further, each day, in order to get into condition after so long a time on the boat. All this was very well, but as each day dawned—and the wind persistedly blew back into the mountains—we became restless, and anxious. Time was disappearing rapidly. We were not accomplishing one of the main reasons for which our expedition had departed from the home port. We certainly did not desire to return without the museum specimens.

In the meantime we were fifteen miles from the boat and fast devouring too large a percentage of our food. We had not planned on quite such enormous appetites. We managed to vary our diet by the desperate means of using sea-gull eggs in omelettes, and roasting one porcupine which, served with carrots, onions and a dash of mustard, tasted not unlike spring lamb. Lack of success—particularly when the wind finally shifted and we commenced hunting in earnest—caused us to realize our hardships in the crude camp where we were never dry, where the incessant winds seemed to all but dash our little tents into the encroaching waves, and where we had begun to crave *fresh meat*. A craving for fresh meat is a steady gnawing sensation that eats away inside of you though you try your best to keep it tamed. There were always trout, yet even of fresh trout out of cool streams we finally sickened.

After big game in Alaska, one hunter usually travels alone with his own guide; or possibly a husband and wife may share a guide. So it is that a writer of Alaskan sport can seldom describe another hunter's experiences. Nor does he know, more than to speak to, another man's guide, yet his own guide is his very best friend. Therefore in Alaska, after bear, there is always only yourself, your own struggles and disappointments, your luck or failure, and the philosophy and ambition of your guide with whom you share all these things.

Thus it was that Mike of medium stature, with a round well-fed stomach, and a twinkle in each brown eye, became my hope for success and my constant daily companion for nearly a month. From Austria he had gone to the United States twenty years before to work in an Ohio coal mine. Thence he drifted, like so many others have drifted, in search of fame or wealth, to Alaska by means of a coal ship, and later as a cod fisherman. Now he managed a steady and respectable living, trapping mink, fox, and land otter during the winter and hoping each summer to find a "sport" to guide.

"Bears," Mike explained to me, "move about 'round four in the morning and lay up during the heat of the day," commencing to appear again towards five in the evening as they wander lazily to the streams for water and to make their supper off of young grass along the banks. So it meant that the chase must continue over a period of twelve or fourteen hours, or else we must not depart from camp until noon, and in this way get only the evening hunt. "Summer very late in coming this year," Mike added apologetically. "Bears travel to Bering Sea side—where they can get food!" . . . We were not near Bering Sea. Always something, I thought, as he offered the excuse. This business of bear hunting was being almost as temperamental as the business of fly fishing for brook trout.

Even the men in the secondary camp, near *The Glory Hole* itself, had no better luck.

"I don't expect to be able to see a bear if one should ever be visible!" I jotted in my journal on our fifth night in camp. "The hunting is so hard and lasts for such a length of time, and what with this climbing up and down high river beds, and steep ridges, the blood seems to pound all over—even in my eyes." And, on the following page, "How will I, in my excitement, remember to raise the rifle from underneath, and not to jerk it—even with an unconscious movement?"

But enough of this. Only two things of any great importance happened in that first location. Rochester got a ten-foot bear and hurried back from the inland camp that same night to tell us. Exciting news! No tidings could have been more welcome and more heartening. Bears and tundra and Pavlof and our tents and the ocean were our complete horizon. We cared nothing for Transatlantic flights, wars in China, or the stock market

—although we had received wireless news daily while still on the *Northern Light.* We cared only about getting bears! . . . those promised beauties for a museum. The second thing of importance was the discovery that our rifles, though well sighted in before leaving the States, all shot low. We wondered whether the atmosphere and the cold were the cause; or whether it was because we were using a different batch of ammunition.

The guides now began to feel that most of us would be "skunked" and the old jealousy increased, fanned by the fact that Nekita's "sport" had bagged a "Bar" as Mike pronounced it. We had, moreover, listened to Larson and Nekita, and taken their advice in regard to choice of hunting grounds. Mike had never been enthusiastic over our decision, but Mike did not have the prestige of the two others. He was not an old-timer in Alaska: ten years ago he had been but a *chechaquo.*

Desperation! . . . John and Albert stepped into our little New England dory and rowed away, bound for the schooner. It had been decided we must change our camp. They expected to make the trip in five hours taking turns at the oars, and would return with the schooner and transport us to fresh hunting grounds. That evening the sun came out for the second time since our arrival at Pavlof Bay. It was greeted by all with waves of arms and loud cheers. Despite the sun, that same night a terrific storm blew up, and lashed shriekingly against our frail shelters. It continued, a raging southeaster, all the next day. Huddled in the cook-tent, fully dressed, we had sat all night; too frightened to push out into the wet teeth of the gale and seek our smaller tents; too frightened to do anything but stay close together and wonder about the small dory that had rowed fifteen miles away. And we remembered, each living breathing second, that the guides had admitted frankly that tents and all might be swept into the bay if the gale should become much worse. To the east and south of us, beyond Pavlof Bay, roared the broad Pacific.

In the morning, when the storm had abated, with the impatience and nervousness of animals flocking out of the ark, we peered forth from the main tent and saw—to our relief—the *Northern Light!* The white ship was riding at anchor in the lee of Ivan Island. We could, at last, pull up stakes and hunt afresh in new territory. Too, we knew the chef would have raisin pies and chocolate cakes. A few good meals before starting again would put vigor into our weary frames.

On June sixth we sailed into Canoe Bay, well protected from the open sea. Once again rain and wind delayed our establishing camp. We had decided it would make better hunting for all if we divided into two parties. By noon of the second day we departed in the launch carrying with us the bare necessities of life in the hunting field. In our party were Frances, John, myself, Robert, Mike, Albert, the steward, and a sailor as cook. This camp was even more open to the elements than the other. One large tent would house the steward and sailor, as well as serve for our kitchen. The guides would make use of a sod *barabara* relic of some trapper. The rest of the expedition would be in camp across the bay.

We discovered a second hunting country that needed, so states my diary: "The agility of an antelope and the endurance of an ox." Spongy niggerheads made walking resemble the leaping of a jumping-jack from one hump to another. Mike and I saw trails of the land otter, mink, and wolverine, several pairs of willow ptarmigan—beautiful birds—hares, and a herd of graceful caribou that permitted us to watch them at close distance for so long as we desired. . . . It is remarkable how quickly even a newcomer in the woods can learn to be alert for all signs of wild life. No bent twig, no bird's nest, no sound did Mike miss, and I soon attuned my own less-sensitive senses to the ways of the wilderness. . . .

It was closed season for caribou. Hungry as we

all were for fresh meat, no one—and we all saw many of these wild shy creatures—used this excuse to take one. The guides had appeased their appetites by broiling bear steaks. Porcupine and sea-gull omelettes were one thing—bear steaks another! Even a continuous diet of salt meat sounded more appetizing.

On our return towards camp on that first night in our new location, Mike and I sat down on an inviting high ridge, to rest. From there we could watch the hair seals disport themselves in the bay, bobbing sleek brown heads out of the rolling grey waves. Mike sauntered off a few yards—scanning every inch of ground at his feet. "*Jeese . . .*" he suddenly cried, with a start. "*Jeese*, Mrs. Borden, look at this. Fresh too! I'd give fifty dollars of my own money to have had you here—when that big fella came out today! . . . must a' been 'leven feet at least." A little later he exclaimed: "You know if we fellas return to King Cove with no *bar* for our sports, the rest of the crowd will have the laugh on us. . . ." The reader must remember that Nekita's sport already had a bear. The rival party was one up.

But the gods decide. Two hours later all was changed. We had reached camp when John and Albert put in a belated appearance over the top of the bluff. Their features in the dim light were barely distinguishable yet we noticed something distinctly springy about their walks, particularly taking into consideration that they had been tramping for some fourteen hours. Yet they both wore the gay air of marching in a parade. Invisible banners were flying.

"Did you get a bear?" Frances and I shouted, being of a certain sex we were not believing what we half suspected. Then we noticed that the late arrivals grinned with a foolish expression resembling the proverbial cat-that-swallowed-the-canary. By this time their loud *yes!*—shouted in answer had not been needed.

Later, when the three of us had devoured hungrily a hot and ample supper of vegetable soup, South American corned-beef, stewed tomatoes, baking powder biscuits with heaping portions of strawberry jam, and a dish of peaches, we oiled the precious rifles—our nightly occupation—and listened to the unfolding of the successful hunt. The two men had found it necessary after once spying the bear to make a broad circle of three or four miles in order that their quarry might not get their scent. After running as fast as they could, crashing through alders and crossing streams, John noticed, fortunately, that the sight of his rifle was out of adjustment. "Just happened to see it as we stopped to make sure the animal was still where we had last seen him an hour before, nibbling at roots . . . then on we ran. And when we got to within range he was right where we figured he would be. . . ."

The remark concerning the rifle sights needs explanation that might be of some use to others contemplating the same experience. It was so damp on the Alaska Peninsula where it rained part of every day that the stocks swelled on all the rifles and we had much difficulty with out sight-adjustments. Most of us had, and liked tremendously, Griffen and Howe Springfields, 30-06, government rifles rebuilt for hunting. They were marvelously balanced and beautiful guns. The Lyman receiver sight itself, the little knob of which rubbed against our trousers as we walked along and would sometimes twist and change the numbering we had taken great pains to set, was what caused us the trouble, not the rifles themselves. Each time prior to taking a shot it became necessary to readjust the knob setting. Since this Alaskan expedition, in 1927, we have changed these rifles for two new Griffen and Howe Springfields with a very much improved peep sight, closer to the eye and a great improvement in every way. This new Griffen and Howe sight when once set cannot get out of proper adjustment. And no rifle could be more satisfactory for Alaskan hunting.

III

At last there was one score for our camp and for the glory of King Cove! It made little difference who had brought it down. We were each one as proud as though the prize had been our own.

"Not as fine a color as I would have liked," John went on, ramming the cleaning rod, and the oiled rag, down into the rifle which had served him well. "But a nine-foot bear."

As we walked, in the cool clear night, towards the two small tents that rose darkly before us, John bantered: "What's the matter with you two girls? With usual women's efficiency you should each have had a bear long before this. . . ."

*   *   *   *

The hard days went by. Each day a long and exhausting tramp; each moment, while out in the field, tense with hope as we scanned through our powerful glasses the surrounding tundra, the foothills of snow-striped mountains, the deep ravines. Each night we climbed into bed and warm sleeping bags—resolving never again would we go after Brown Bear, but eight hours later not wishing to waste a second before getting started—just one more try. And soon my daily notes repeated over and over, "Oh . . . if I could only *see* a Brown Bear!" On the open sweep of land between the steep mountain sides, and the bay, we could—except in a pouring rain—have spotted one several miles away. But for Frances and Robert, for Mike and me, no bear appeared.

"Too bad you and Miss Ames don't see no *bars*," Mike would sympathize. "And you give him good looks—too! Well," he would then drawl philosophically, "maybe we run across one some time." Mike, as he would perch on the vantage point of a high bank overlooking a descending valley, and give the bear "good looks," resembled a well-nourished pouter pigeon. Yet he was strong as a bear. Packing me across the swiftest and deepest streams seemed to him no effort whatsoever. In fact he often boasted concerning the number of "fat sports" for whom he had done the same.

Robert and Mike became two more and more discouraged guides as the season drew to a close. And there was rain, interminable rain. The tents became all but unendurable, and the blankets even in our sleeping bags were seldom dry. Yes, that other little camp which stood near the Illinois River, and from where we went mallard-shooting with old Bill, was in our memory a bit of luxurious living.

One night a bear of nine or ten feet in length, judging from his sprawling footprints, passed close

to the guides *barabara*. He had perhaps smelled
the food in the cook-tent and came down to look
us over. Another time John spied a bear and two
cubs on a mountain side several miles away from
where he hunted. So small they appeared from
afar that he and Albert claimed they looked like
a squirrel strolling with a couple of chipmunks.
And still another time he saw a huge black male
but as luck would have it the wind was blowing
back into the mountains which made almost an
impossible approach. In order to attain a distance
within rifle range of him the men would have had
to climb up and over a nearby mountain, and come
down toward the bear from the topmost peak of
the same mountain on which the animal stood,
already turning his head suspiciously this way and
that.

How the other camp was faring, we knew little.
One morning we saw a sailor cross the bay, carrying them a fresh supply of provisions from the
schooner. He then rowed back to us, with the
message that Mrs. Slaughter had brought down,
after stalking him for five miles, a magnificent
male. Good for her! It was marvelous news.

June seventeenth! Frances got a large female
with a fine dark skin, far better than the only bear
so far taken by our little party.

Hunting the Great Brown Bear

June eighteenth—only three more days of hunting!—the sun rose at quarter past one. A perfect morning. And for the first time, on arising, we saw the tops of the snow-covered mountains encircling Canoe Bay. Heretofore, we had had no conception of their stern and austere beauty.

And on this day of days the narrator of all these many disheartening weeks, of rain and physical exhaustion, finally caught sight of a Brown Bear and never will she forget what followed. Though most readers may feel an aversion for big-game hunting tales replete with the unattractive pronoun, I ran, I fell, I pulled the trigger, you will have to forgive me for concluding an already too long story by describing the most serious, the most thrilling, and at the same time as comic a two hours as I can ever remember.

It was seven o'clock. Mike and I had already tramped for five solid hours. The thermometer had risen to seventy in the sunlight and while it was hot and hard going on the flats, a cold wind whistled through us as we reached the higher ridges; a wind that had passed over snow-capped mountains. Advancing a few yards we stopped and studied thoroughly every inch of ground ahead, hoping, as always, that we would discover *Ursus gyas* wandering from an alder patch into the open or returning to the protection of another patch of these dwarf alders. But it was now getting late and we still had a three-hour tramp before supper and bed.

Suddenly Mike whispered excitedly, speaking very clearly, "Mrs. Borden—there's a *bar!*" According to my diary, "I grabbed him on the shoulder and couldn't say a word!" But Mike said, *"God help us."*

The bear was at least two miles away and running down a knoll—towards where we had no idea. For he was quickly out of sight. The next problem was how to find him again. We knew this entailed arduous tramping and an uphill climb back over the very territory we had just covered, all of the time trying to figure out where the wary creature had gone.

Mike quickly assumed the lead, handing me my rifle which he had been carrying. Shell in chamber, but on safe, it was now ready for a hurried shot. Tired as we already were we proceeded to stalk that illusive beast for an hour and a half without ever catching sight of him. I can see us now as we clambered from one ridge to another and peered down hopefully into each yawning valley. The spongy niggerheads tripped my aching legs every few yards; the loaded rifle sprawled out from under me. But Mike never knew. He was far too intent on his search to so much as turn round. And I continued to repeat over and over in my exhausted brain, with the persistent beating of a metronome, "My only chance, my only chance, my only chance. My first big game. My first and only chance."

Finally we found him. At the side of a swift mountain stream. He was still running, that huge brown beast we were searching for so frantically. Between us and the wild animal, fortunately, rose a high bank with alders along the top. Ploughing further through the dense brush we followed, noiselessly as possible, but this was not quite possible. Of a sudden the bear turned his head, glanced up, caught sight of us, stopped. But keeping his head turned inquisitively in our direction. He was almost out of range, certainly a long shot. Since he had not as yet caught our scent, he was still uncertain what we were.

"Now—*shoot!*" came from Mike, the sound tearing through his teeth. "Steady!" . . .

Steady in an off-hand position with shaking legs, puffing breath, and eyes dimmed by a pounding heart? Impossible! Nevertheless I tried to remember the lessons . . . deliberately the rifle came up from underneath the bear, up, up, until the sight covered his great legs.

Then to squeeze the trigger.

Bang . . . I had shot. . . . And missed.

"Steady . . ." once more hissed Mike.

Again—gently squeeze the trigger. . . . "Don't jerk it!" sang through my dizzy consciousness.

This time the bear was knocked down, turned a complete somersault, and before the magazine could be reloaded, had dashed through alders and disappeared—out of sight around a bend in the river.

"Never mind—you done good!" sympathized Mike when he saw his companion mightily close to tears. Her one chance. She had muffed it. Then he instructed me to keep the rifle loaded in case of a sudden attack. We were, it appeared, to run in the wake of the wounded animal that carried the flesh wound of a powerful bullet: a 220 grain semi exposed soft point cartridge put out by the Western Cartridge Company. (As these are no longer made we would today use the short exposed or half exposed soft point Western Cartridge.)

Mike soon outdistanced me, and was far ahead. Hat shoved on to the back of his head, heels flying, he let out into a sprint with all he had in him; forgetting any one or anything behind him, and completely intent on finding some trace of the escaping game. It was almost dark. Storm clouds gathered over the darkening mountains. A strong wind blew into our faces. After we had gone ahead blindly for half a mile, and Mike had disappeared from sight, I dropped down on to the moss-covered ground to catch up on breath; and worried for fear I would not be able to move even though the enraged beast might appear—and attack.

After a few undescribable minutes which seemed a whole eternity Mike reappeared from behind some alders, wiping his forehead with a large red bandanna handkerchief, and himself blowing like a porpoise.

"Too bad—we lost him!" he panted.

So on we tramped. Life was hard. Mike and I were respectively, Chairman of the Board and President of a business that had failed.

Two miles further Mike decided he would peer into the center of a certain alder patch. Still he had not given up a faint hope of reviving our chances to return successful. Failure—complete— would be a disgrace. He hunted for any possible signs of blood. "If he's sick he'll lie down in alders. If not hurt bad—we'll never find him," Mike explained as he turned off towards the low-growing brush.

In another second he spun round on his heel. His face, as he wheeled, worked into unreadable contortions.

"Look!" he yelled. "Look!" he yelled again,

this time waving one hand. "He's in there trying to get up. But he's too sick. Don't get scared. Take your time—and shoot!"

A huge brown mass became plainly discernible, thrashing on the ground. In a moment we could distinguish a large head, fore-legs struggling to rise to its feet with effort. A horrible moment. A sickening moment overburdened with the strangely conflicting emotions of pity and a desire for immediate self-preservation. The Museum was forgotten. I had wounded a wild animal that might attack. If I did not get him first—maybe. . . . The guides had all warned of this.

"Hurry, Mrs. Borden—here he comes. . . ."

Some inner something caused me to raise the rifle, steadily, and aim at the same moment as the crippled bear—looking absolutely enormous—emerged from the alders. The shot found its mark. I have never known why because I was far too frightened to know anything. The bullet had penetrated the vital organs behind the left foreleg. It was not unlike sinking, by accident, a long putt on the eighteenth green.

Mike, I think, had begun to dance up and down. So had I.

"Gee ain't that great? Ain't that great?" . . . he finally exploded. "Now the other guys won't have the laugh on me!"

Then he ran towards the prize.

"Come on over—he's deader than a corpse!" he called back. "That sure is a swell bullet. . . . Look at the hole it tore open the first time. . . ."

I followed. The poor creature would have died during the night if we had not tracked him to the lonely spot where he had hoped to escape the two hunters who had so mercilessly cut short his life. The raw tear of the powerful cartridge would have caused him to bleed to death.

Again conflicting emotions. I could not decide whether to laugh—or cry.

Instead, over the large brown carcass, Mike and I shook hands long and hard.

VII

"Four Thousand Walrus"

DURING THE TIME we hunted Brown Bear on the Peninsula those of us who had never seen Bering Sea—and the Arctic beyond—felt an increasing curiosity concerning The Far North fasten itself upon our minds. . . . What would the Land of the Midnight Sun, with its almost mythical romance, be like to visit in real life? What Arctic mammals would we take to form a scientific group for study, as well as for a museum case? Would we actually see, in its icy natural habitat, the Great White King of the North? Such were a few of the many questions on which we pondered while we were not entirely engrossed with the *Ursus gyas* and the problems he presented.

When the last day of hunting came to a close we weighed anchor, preparing to leave our guides at King Cove and proceed on our way. The wonder in all our hearts being—how far would we penetrate toward the top of the world?

We, of the so-called gentle sex, had changed considerably from the timid four who had in April set sail from San Francisco. Often we discussed, in a quiet and matter of fact manner, a possible disaster either due to shoals in Bering Sea or by being crushed in Arctic ice, and planned what we must do should the emergency arise, but with not half so much heated interest as when we talked of the fresh beef which we expected to buy on our arrival in Unalaska. Hunger for fresh meat was upon us. Catastrophes merely a possibility.

Westward we steamed, to Dutch Harbor. Then, into Bering Sea. Up, up, bound ultimately towards our goal marked on the globe the preceding winter of our preparation; where, "We'll hunt walrus and polar bears up there in the ice pack. . . . Do you think you can make it?"

At Nome we waved good-bye regretfully to the two members of our party, Bobsey and Barney, who had known from the beginning they could not longer be away. And here in Nome we took on two new passengers, two Eskimo hunters who came to be our guides while hunting in the ice. To their temporary summer village, on the beach outside the town, we had gone to find them, in the company of Tom Ross of the Coast Guard Service, a friend who was also friendly with these shy little people. There we had laid the matter before the chief of The King Island Eskimos. After an excited all-night pow-wow indulged in by every male member of the tribe the two hunters had decided to accept our invitation. Departing from wives and children, sailing so far away, would indeed be a hardship since these particular Eskimos were model husbands and fathers. Yet the temptation of a hunt among ice flows, and with an important expedition for a "mooziem," had proved too strong.

John Katungazuk, "Big John" we called him, was older than "me frien'" John Ugikuna, and reputed to be the island's mightiest hunter. He had already brought down fourteen polar bears. These bears being the Eskimo's most dreaded enemy, a man's hunting prowess was judged greatly by the number of these mighty creatures the hunter could kill. "Little John," on the other hand, was deemed second best hunter. His score—so far—five polar bears.

The King Islanders dwell each winter on a small and sheer rocky island in the North of Bering Sea. From this remote stronghold they are removed to Nome each summer by the Revenue Cutter at the instructions from the Government in order that during July and August they may have the opportunity to make a few dollars in cash working as longshoremen and selling their carved ivory. At King Island they always leave harpoons, and kyaks, having no use for them while in the "City." So there, the night after setting sail from Nome, we dropped anchor in order that the two Johns might fully prepare themselves for the eventful weeks to come.

We followed them ashore. We struggled up the slippery grey boulders on hands and knees, puffingly out of breath, while our guides hopped from one to another and reached the high vantage point where were situated their houses with the speed and surefootedness of a pair of goats. They had the audacity to turn round, and laugh at our efforts. And it was here, at King Island, that we were asked to admire the skulls of Big John's polar bears. Dangling beside the doorway of his primitive hut hanging over the sea, or so it seemed, were the grisly hollow-eyed trophies that swayed at the end of a rope like a batch of dried fish.

"Look—*Me* Polar Bears!" he had cried as he took the fourteen of them down off the hook and jingled them on their string before our eyes. They were so dried and crisp and deathlike that it was hard to say "How beautiful!" or "How marvellous!"

"Polar Bear kill 'em lots Eskimo!" he told us, his alive black eyes filled with the memories of each hunt.

July fourteenth we crossed the Arctic Circle, bound for the waters North of the northernmost coast of Siberia. We were expecting to find walrus

there, between the mainland and Wrangel Island
in the ice pack, since hunting these mammals in
the Alaskan Arctic to the East was closed except to
natives. The white schooner shrouded by fog
that circled her like a low wreath of smoke, we
steered bravely north and westward into the Great
Polar Ocean. We had been forced to put all
thoughts of those dear to us at home, and our
moral obligations towards them, out of our minds,
and deeper into our hearts, in the intense business
of reaching the farthest North humanly possible
by ship; and later to return to the States with the
promised specimens. Hadn't the whaling skipper
anticipated that we would see "four thousand walrus to one brown bear!"

As we sailed, under engine and canvas, on our
designated course, we thus put civilization and
our earthly contacts farther and farther behind us
. . . too far to be able to return quickly even had
the necessity arisen. We had assumed this awe-
some responsibility when we left the house, and
closed the door.

As we crossed the Arctic Circle large flocks of
murres and guillemots flashed by, darting towards
the Siberian Shore. Out of the fog came a flock
of King Eider drakes.

On the fifteenth—I note the date because the
element of time was as vital in the Siberian Arctic

as it was during the period we hunted brown bear, in the Arctic the season for navigation being of but a few weeks duration—the fog had lifted and we sat lazily on deck, reading and writing and listening to the strains from a portable victrola. The two Eskimos never ceased playing this machine for one minute, except to go below for food. They tried both sides of a fairly sizable collection of records, and confided that the "Philippines," meaning the Hawaiian selections, were their favorites.

The Diesel engines continued to throb smoothly; today the sails had been furled. And at the same time we were pleasantly conscious of the odor of freshly baked cookies, and coffee simmering in a pot. The French chef, temperamental though he was, knew well how to tickle our palates when not suffering from *mal de mer*.

Now and then, while watching float past us a succession of fantastic shapes of drift-ice, we would forget the romances and adventures of the Past about which we were reading, and steep ourselves instead with the thrill of the moment itself: the shimmering sun, the endless, dazzling sea, the painted ice, and the queer strange loneliness. Phantom ships, ghosts of the doomed ones which had been caught in the ice in the approximate latitude and longitude in which we now cruised, seemed once more to be riding the waves in the full glory of their square-rigged spars.

Yet, while on deck snuggled warmly under steamer blankets, and clad in heavy parkas and mukluks in preparation for a possible hunt, we revelled in the fact that we had actually left the coast line of Arctic Siberia behind and were already but eleven hundred miles from the Pole.

This ice round our boat, which jammed now and then against the wooden hull sheathed with iron bark, was merely the fringe. Not much further away we would encounter the great pack itself. On this loose ice, however, we expected to find walrus. On the edge of the pack—the polar bears.

We were, we knew, the first ship of the year to pass through Bering Strait. We might be the only one—during the whole of the short navigable season. Any trouble—and there could be no aid. The close horizon held us prisoner within a wide blue disinterested dome. Nothing can be less personal, less a part of you than sea and sky. Land—all land save desert land—is friendly. The sea is alien.

I mention all this since our emotions, our hopes and fears, were constantly stirred up within us. We had no outlet. We could not get away from the Arctic, and ourselves. We had known, since leaving home, cold, and seasickness; we had even hazarded our own safety in rescuing a distressed trader pounding on rocks in Bering Sea; we had known real fear for our own ship; we had known moments of homesickness and longings for the luxuries of civilization and comforts of home. What we saw, and what we felt, concerned us as matters of the utmost importance in all of the world.

In the meantime, the two Eskimos, busy with the victrola, appeared quite impervious to the odor of freshly baked cookies that was so tempting to the rest of us. Perhaps, this aroma was too new in their lives. At any rate they were frankly hungry for a generous slice of walrus steak broiled over their own home fires. Despite the excitement of their importance on board they were, at first, lonesome for home, and rather wistfully mentioned their wives and babies.

Shortly after lunch Little John was pulled aloft by means of the bosun's chair and stood in the crow's nest, like Balboa surveying his whereabouts from a peak in Darien. Below him, Big John strolled back and forth on deck, his keen eyes alert for any signs of walrus on drifting ice. He waited, too, the signal from the man above.

Of a sudden—the man in the crow's nest commenced to shout wildly and clap his hands.

"Cap'n — Cap'n — Look. . . . Walrus!" he

managed to holler loud enough so that his voice would carry down to us below.

We saw that even Big John had begun to wave his arms in the general direction of starboard. Then the navigator walked out from the chart room in the stern. He stood, staring off to starboard. . . . Something had happened. We in the deck chairs tossed aside encumbering blankets, hopped to our feet, and grabbed for binoculars. It was then we spied the objects of the native's noisy excitement. Out there on the Arctic Ocean, so beautiful, so calm, floated ice on which lay hundreds of walrus. Though from our distance they looked like nothing real, nothing alive, merely red shapeless dabs on their cold white beds.

We had reached the home waters of the comic ivory-pronged herd concerning which so many stories of childhood have been written. Here were the monsters who had attacked Nansen and overturned his boat. Here were the absurd looking creatures whose valuable hide and blubber and ivory is sought by natives of both the Siberian and Alaskan coasts.

"If you happen to get into the big herd itself, I understand you can see thousands of them," John Borden put in as he approached. He, being master and navigator, had been taking a sight and verifying *The Northern Light's* position. Then he left us to speak with the one-time whaling skipper, on this voyage his right-hand man.

We overheard him, a moment later, give orders to lower the launch. And at the same instant bells tinkled from the pilot house to the engine room. The engines were being signalled off. We were to drift.

Pandemonium reigned. The entire crew had hurried on deck to see why, so abruptly, the engines had been shut off. And the walrus were drifting closer. The wind, from off the ice, fortunately carried our scent in the opposite direction from the animals we were about to stalk. Everything was in readiness but ourselves and some of us had had all day to prepare for just this event.

Guns, shells, kodaks, were all below deck, as well as the necessary white parkas for hunting Arctic game. Soon, however, we clambered back up the steep companionway, out of breath from haste and excitement, and slightly disorganized for a novel pursuit never before attempted.

The launch had already been lowered. The Eskimos waited by the ladder, impatiently, politely. Both carried harpoons.

A second later the five of us in our party, as well as two Eskimo guides, and the second mate to run the boat, were off. The crew waved good-bye from the deck where they stood leaning over the rail, curious as to the outcome.

We advanced in the direction of a fairly substantial hummock of ice to which we were to anchor. Behind us towed two kyaks, lashed together side by side. They were to be the further means of approach to the walrus themselves.

We shoved up to a large cake rising and falling with the slight swell, and drifting with the current. The mate heaved out the anchor. It held fast.

The natives drew the kyaks alongside the launch. They too were clad in white. Their excited little faces looked strangely brown in contrast to their white hoods, and the white ice, while their eyes stared out, unusually black.

Cautiously first Big John, then Little John, crawled down into the two forward cockpits of the small canoe-like crafts. They beckoned for a hunter to follow. After the usual argument: "You go. . . . No, you." Rochester followed, taking the seat between the two cockpits in the stern.

The Eskimos pulled the hoods of their white drill garments further over their heads, nearly covering their faces. So did the man in the stern.

Off they skimmed over the water. I can see

them now. Down on them played a brilliant Northern sun as they glided noiselessly over the Arctic Ocean as serenely calm as a mountain lake, all but for a gentle swell. By means of the graceful rise and fall of two small paddles, they were being propelled towards a particular floe upon which lay fifteen or twenty walrus.

Breathlessly we in the launch, anchored to an ice cake, watched. We knew Rochester to be a fine rifle shot! One of the best. Surely, before many more minutes elapsed one member of our party would procure a trophy—and the natives their meat! Frankly, it looked so easy that we were inclined to somewhat pooh pooh the importance devoted to walrus hunts in volumes of Arctic travel. We would not only take specimens for the museum, but a trophy apiece, and before the day was done.

What stupid beasts they were to sleep so soundly with danger so close!

At just that instant the reddish-brown creatures on the ice apparently reached the same conclusion. One by one they raised their heads, and their funny flat faces turned to right and left. Suspiciously they sniffed the air, cast their tiny eyes— for such huge bulks!—to every side in search of an encroaching enemy.

As their agitation increased, and perhaps because lacking any better way to display emotion, they proceeded to dig sharp white ivory into the tough hide of their friend closest by.

Meanwhile the small boat stood still. Like three white statues the men sat, motionless.

A few minutes later the mammoth beasts were once more fast asleep. Either, like most fat human beings, their nerves were well-upholstered and not prone to worry for long at a time; or else they had perceived the approaching object and decided it was just another cake of drifting ice. Whatever they thought, they were once more in the peaceful land of nod.

Why, with thousands of ice-pans to choose from, had they reserved for their use such a silly ivory-soap cake to float upon? Stupid creatures, indeed. Too stupid to even bother and hunt.

Once more the intrepid three skimmed ahead. Again we waited.

This time they were able to edge up to a distance of about twenty-five yards. Still the walrus slumbered.

Since there was no firm enough cake of ice on to which they could conveniently crawl, it was necessary to shoot from the kyak.

We saw our hunter load his magazine. At the same instant the quarry awoke. Once more they peered about them.

"Four Thousand Walrus"

Bang.

Every animal on that floe of ice hurtled itself into the sea.

When the reverberation of the shot had crashed round the horizon and returned to the spot from where it was fired, there was, in the near or far distance, not a single walrus to be seen upon any pan of ice. Instead, almost instantaneously, the three men who went to sea in a small boat became the center of an attacking army of snorting and infuriated beasts. How dared the hunters have penetrated their icy fastness! Spouts of water blew like fountains out of their faces, tail flippers whisked menacingly. The water was thick with the enormous bodies which somersaulted in and out of the waves, flashing their long white tusks.

Although perhaps strictly speaking the men in the kyaks were in no violent danger, yet one very possible dig of two angry tusks into the side of the frail canoes, and over they would go.

The Eskimos raised their harpoons, ready, if necessary. And the man in the stern, with his rifle, prepared for a possible attack.

But the excitement subsided. Gradually the great beasts decided to withdraw, snorting as they went; and the canoes turned, gliding back over the way they had gone.

Stupid beasts, we had thought. But not so stupid. Easy hunting, we had thought. But not so easy.

And perhaps it will seem incredible to believe that we staged another equally unsuccessful hunt. My John—to distinguish him from the Eskimo Johns—tried his hand and once more, each huge object threshed into the sea.

Something was certainly wrong. We must find out. The Eskimos themselves could not explain except, what we already knew, that a walrus when dead, sinks. If not killed instantly the contraction of his muscles causes his great body to slide off the quaintly small piece of ice on which he is ordinarily found.

The outlook, from a humane point of view even more than the idea of our own stupidity, was a depressing one, to say the least. For blood had spurted from the neck of each of the two walrus shot, and they would perhaps die.

Had our shells not been powerful enough? This, I will reply to later.

We turned to our books for references. Scull, in his *Hunting in Alaska and the Arctic*, described several attempts similar to ours, until he finally discovered that a shot aimed at the ear would reach a vulnerable place where death could be dealt instantaneously. One inch to right or left and the game was lost. But the ear cannot be seen without benefit of a microscope.

*   *   *   *

The following morning—our schooner having been piloted during the night a few miles distant from the heavy ice—we again hoped for better luck. Cruising northwest, winding in and out between floes, I carried the daily record on deck and jotted down: "Walrus hunting is a snare and delusion!"

Murres and parasitic jaegers, the latter vultures of the Arctic, followed in our wake. While out at sea ice crystals glimmered in the bright sun like square-cut diamonds. Above, puffy white clouds sailed like white ships on their own smooth sea.

While we in the aft-cabin had slept, a tiny song bird lighted on deck, exhausted after a long flight. The boys on watch had gathered him up in their hands and given him food and drink. I believe they expected to make a pet of him. But the small dark creature, with a splash of red feathers on the back of his head, was more frightened of the strange hands than of the doubtful prospects of finding again the land about which he had been so mistaken when he flew down to rest. Off he fluttered, first to the top of the rail; and before too many hands could reach forth he had lifted his wings and was gone.

Just as lunch was announced, the Eskimos, who continually kept watch, cried out the exciting word:—"Walrus!"

Lunch must wait. Every one of us were now "hell bent" on bagging one of these illusive mammals.

There being but two male hunters it was again Rochester's turn. The men must be successful before we three women could think of asking to try our luck. This time no launch was lowered and we watched from the deck. Thank goodness, all went well. An hour or so later a two-ton walrus, by means of windlass and halliards, and the aid of five of the crew, was hauled on to the forward deck. The U. M. C. Remington delayed mushroom cartridge had penetrated at a spot exactly twelve inches back of the eye.

Odobenus divergens. A species considerably larger, quite distinct and unconnected with the Atlantic Walrus, *Odobenus rosmarus.* According to the second mate, who had seen in the Kara Sea many herds of walrus, the Atlantic species were so much smaller they might almost be the young of these mammoths of the Siberian Arctic.

"That big boy 'bout hundred fifty year old!"

"Four Thousand Walrus"

Big John explained, with the inborn knowledge of the natives of Arctic wastes. We were all standing by while careful scientific measurements were being taken. "Walrus some time eat duck. Lots duck find 'em stomach. . . . And . . . and what you call 'em shellfish." Then he added that the wild ducks, bluebills mostly, were caught while in the eclipse and not able to fly.

The engines were turning over. Signals from the pilot house. The course would be nor' nor' east towards Herald Shoal.

While listening to the series of bells and hearing once more the pound of the two faithful engines, I could not help but wonder about the life and habits of this giant beast. A hundred and fifty years old! Born when the ink on the Declaration of Independence had scarcely dried. And what had he accomplished, in all that time? How much ground had he covered—in a century and a half, the span of six generations of man? . . . How different from the beautiful and fragile little Arctic bird who had by chance landed on our deck. A life-time of a few months, and in that short span he would travel perhaps twenty thousand miles, perhaps forty, who knows, really.

"Imagine a big lump like that being fastidious enough to choose nothing but the delicacies of the world—wild duck and shellfish!" some one commented with a laugh. "No wonder he has lived so long!"

Lewis Carrol missed a few tricks when Alice did not have the pleasure of dining with a gentleman of such tastes.

In comparison we were about to proceed towards our own table where soup had been waiting for over two hours, and where we would be offered a platter of warmed-up beef stew from out of a can. However, the steward had mumbled something cheering—about the chef having baked a fresh chocolate cake.

*   *   *   *

That night, after a successful afternoon, both men now had their trophy—we remained on deck to see the Midnight Sun dip to the horizon, whirling like a red top, only to rise slowly again into the sky. The birth of a new day on the most northerly ocean of the world was a sight we shall never forget. The pageantry of it all was as fantastic as though we were living in pages of Jules Verne. And how few of those who have never seen the Arctic Sea could ever believe its amazing power and beauty!

Leaving the colorful scene above deck we climbed down the companionway, planning before retiring to make waffles on the small electric waffle-iron and intending at the same time to ascertain—once and for all!—whether any one else would have a chance to bring home a walrus head: —meaning, of course, that it was the three female members of the expedition who had begun to wonder. We were just commencing to sense the fact that no one else expected us to.

"No!" said the head of my family firmly as he sat down to cut his fork into the succulent, though crisp dainties which had been placed before him. "Certainly you can't! It's much too dangerous. . . . The natives get so excited they might easily turn the boat over. What then? . . ." He laid down his fork. "Supposing you're attacked? What would you do?"

We dropped the subject for a few moments. The smell of waffles hovered in the comfortable cabin. Perhaps we were trading on the fact that a man was weakest on a full stomach. At any rate we bided our time.

Then the other wife took courage. "Couldn't we try? We'll be careful. . . . Anyway, we couldn't do very much worse than you and John did yesterday—" and she laughed.

But her answer, as well, was firmly in the negative.

If you have never had an argument with a husband on the subject of his wife going walrus hunting, you cannot conceive how violent such an argument may become. Whether we would be permitted to try was, to us at the moment, of utmost importance. As far as we were concerned our entire point of view from then on, until the end of the voyage, would depend on it. We had accepted side by side with the rest of them the risk and hazards of sailing that northern latitude, and the many discomforts. Now we each coveted a fair chance to compete in the bringing home of a prize in search of which we had voyaged thousands of adventurous miles.

Even the waffles did not win our point. It was not until nine o'clock the next morning when a voice shouted down the companion way—"All ready, the rest of you, for hunting! Hurry up— Game won't wait!"—that we realized our opportunity had come.

And that *was* excitement! As luck would have it Frances had caught cold and decided she had better remain in bed. Illness was something we all dreaded so she would have to trust to another chance.

The two who were left—tossed a coin. And I won. By the time we had reached deck the Eskimos were waiting, ready, with beaming smiles wreathing their honest little faces. "King Island ladies—no shoot good!" admitted Little John with rather a foolish grin. "They too scairt." Whereupon he gave Big John a knowing smile.

While stepping down into the kyak I listened to a few husbandly directions flung at me as John handed down the Springfield, shells, and the camera which I insisted on taking. Such as:— "Don't move or you'll tip the boat over. Don't point your gun at one of the Eskimos. Don't try and walk on the ice without the natives holding you by the arm. And," lastly, "don't get excited and step backward into the ocean." Probably many others, but we were gliding away now from the big boat, were rounding the stern, were heading in the direction of walrus a quarter of a mile away.

The sea was smooth and day overcast. Seated in that tiny boat, barely rising above the water's cold grey surface, able to reach out and dangle my fingers—which of course I did not dream of doing after the many instructions—in the Arctic Ocean, was a sensation more thrilling than I had ever imagined possible while watching the hunts of others. The ice pans, from our lowly position, seemed high and wobbly and dangerous. What if you tried to climb on one—and it rolled over. . . .

The Eskimos, close ahead of me, were chattering like a pair of magpies. Agilely our little craft threaded its way between ice cakes with the lightness of a feather. First Big John would stand up—and this was frightening!—then Little John, in order to better see the floe on which lay the four beasts we were stalking so silently. "The natives get so excited they might easily turn the boat over. . . . What then? . . ." Perhaps my husband was right.

"Do what we do!" the two guides now fairly hissed over their shoulders, as they crouched low over the bow. "They wake!" came again. We halted, and lay very still.

Then on we paddled.

As in the bear hunt, because of the combination of my own doubtful ability and the danger we were in, I felt cold all over and my heart pounded even in my forehead. We were circling, trying to conceal ourselves behind some fairly high ice. The ever present swell, sucking in and out from under the spongy edges, was breaking against the side of the pan which my guides pointed to as the very one on to which we were expected to climb.

Somehow, I managed to crawl on hands and knees from the tippy boat onto the equally tippy ice. And there we were. . . . Nothing under us save a few yards of bobbing ice—small as a cork in all that vast expanse of sea—to guard us from twenty-six fathoms of icy ocean. So slippery was the ice that it was all we could do to hold any position once we had assumed it. And nothing to cling to—should any of us three start slipping. I shall never forget the sensation!

Little John nodded his head towards the game —not so far away. And when I looked up I realized to my horror that we were on the identical cake of ice on which huddled the four mammoth walrus. The ice, banked directly ahead of us, saved us, where we kneeled, from being seen. But I could perceive enough to know that the animals had already sensed our nearness—were commencing to toss their tusks up and back, restlessly, as though they were about to shove off.

The guides had been watching the situation with the eyes of those who depend on their skill for all the necessities of their lives, food, clothes, fuel, and skins for their boats.

"Shoot 'em!" whispered Little John.

Twelve inches back of the eye . . . the ear was there. We had found it by measurement. Twelve inches back of the eye . . . just twelve inches! . . . I was trying to get the sight to hold steady enough.

"Shoot 'em!" reiterated Little John. "They go."

Conscious that both knees were soaking wet and balance anything but secure, I did what I was told.

And all went well. Three disappeared but one remained.

The pleasure of the moment seemed to be as much the Eskimos' as it was mine.

"I felt little bit sick," Little John now tried to explain with a hearty smile and a big shake of his small hand, "when Cap'n Borden said ladies no shoot 'em walrus. Walrus easy!"

Two hours later Rochester's wife had equally good luck. Better luck, because the tusks of her trophy were longer and better shaped than mine.

And what fun we did have when we sat round the supper table, like all hunters anywhere in the world, talking it all over.

The two men had laughed a little self-consciously, we three decided privately among ourselves, after they had gone on deck to smoke, when we teased them about how difficult it was to bag a walrus! . . .

VIII

White King of the North

WHEN THE MEASUREMENTS had been duly taken of the enormous warty hides and noted on the museum chart, they were packed in salt, and laid away in dories to remain until we should enter the Golden Gate. That same night a gale blew down from the North, driving us before it. To the coast of Siberia we headed until the storm should subside.

From then on, from the evening of July sixteenth until the morning of August eleventh—nearly four weeks—we sailed Arctic Seas, bearing the brunt of wind and waves and ice. We had set for ourselves a standard to achieve and nothing would turn us back until we had done all possible to reach Wrangel Island where, on the broken ice off shore, we felt certain we would find the Polar Bears.

"I've sailed into the Arctic north of Bering Strait every summer for forty years and have seen only one Polar Bear," we had been told at Unalaska by the Captain of a famous cutter now sailing the seas no more. This, though discouraging, did not mean we were going in the pursuit of the hopeless: for, on the contrary, those on the few ships who had managed to penetrate the ice and fog circling Wrangel Island, had always seen the white creatures for which we now searched.

"Ice ahead!" . . . had of late become an announcement we had learned to fear. Because it usually implied that seas were rough and this was ice from the Arctic jam, reaching across thousands of miles just beyond us. The current here, if we should become enclosed—not like the Greenland current which would eventually carry a ship south to open water and freedom—would carry us on, north and west, never to return.

Well do I recall one early morning, between two and three. Most of us in the aft cabins were in bed, but not my partner. He was on watch. The night was bitterly cold, bitterly damp. I had hopped into a heap of blankets, fortified by all my clothes.

Engines were being signalled off. Excited shouts of men carried through the two round brass-ringed portholes opening onto deck. "Ice . . . Ice . . ." could be plainly overheard. Jumping out of bed, and after pulling on one more parka over all else, I climbed back up the stairs, back to the wind-swept deck where we had stood watching all day and most of the night.

"What are you doing here?" demanded John

when he saw me. "You'll catch your death of cold!"

"What is it? Why were the engines shut off?"

And John turned, pointed towards the port side, off the port bow.

"Wrangel Island is there," he said.

The Eskimos approached, their coffee-colored faces solemn, afraid, I thought. They, too, had never been so far away from home. In treacherous water we were. And we all knew how treacherous.

Big John fastened the cord of his reindeer parka closer round his neck and smacked his small gloved hands against his chest. At that moment we jammed against an enormous berg. The boat shuddered. The masts groaned. We tried not to catch one another's eye.

"Maybe Polar Bear . . . Wrangel Island," Big John managed to enunciate, after a minute, trying to smile because he had noticed the frightened face that must have been peering from out my own white hood.

I had seen threatening wind clouds scurrying above the masts, and, down below the ship's rail a grey and billowing sea. More hummocks of dirty ice—ice that had obviously cracked off from some nearby shore—slammed against *The Northern Light*, split in two, and drifted on. They reminded me of evil faces seen in a crowd of human beings, faces that we were glad to watch move on out of sight.

"What chance do you think we have of finding a break in this drift ice?" the navigator was asking of Captain Joe who stood close beside him, hands behind his back in the attitude usually assumed by men who have spent years at sea.

"You can't tell yet," came the answer from the white-haired sailor who had, as well, never sailed where we sailed on that serious night.

We were but four or five miles off the coast of Wrangel Island. When we reached the northwest point of the partially obscured land we came upon a solid ice-field, leading off into the forbidding distance as far as the eye could see.

"Too big a sea!" said John as the two men discussed what to do. "We couldn't hunt bears—if we saw any."

Boldly we cruised back and forth along the edge of the impenetrable ice, searching for a chance to break through. But no chance came.

We began to pitch from side to side. The wind increased in strength.

The schooner changed its course. . . . Once more we were obliged to head South. Once more to bide our time.

"Have a cup of coffee—madam?" It was the steward's voice. Muffled in a grey wool hood and cloak he appeared above the companion hatch. "It's nice and 'ot and do you good!"

This was August sixth. Five days later, the morning of the eleventh, our longed-for, fought-for goal was reached at last. Wrangel Island now lay close off the bow, to port. Unimpeded we cruised in the glistening morning sunshine, alongside the drift ice near shore. It was here—surely—that we would find—him—whom we sought.

Tensely, dark glasses protecting our eyes from snow blindness, we scanned every inch, every floe, every jagged berg.

"*Polar Bears!*" peeled out the two Eskimos' voices. "*Polar Bears!*" they reiterated, their voices ascending higher each time.

"Look at them. . . . They just stand there . . ." cried out one of our party.

Not even the Brown Bear, giant that he was, gave us the thrill which we felt upon seeing for the first time this really magnificent giant of icy wastes. The two white beasts upon whom we feasted our gaze were huge, almost incredibly so. Nonchalantly they strolled along their white trail wobbling their long necks to right and left, rearing their heads, their black noses sniffing the air. They spied us—as clearly as we spied them. They could not get our scent, because of an off-shore breeze, so therefor had not the slightest conception as to what the white ship, and the black figures on her decks might mean. Nevertheless, in fullest admiration we watched their every move. And we thought of the golden-white floor-rugs in palaces of the Czars, in great houses of England, in New York apartments.

This pair—males both—were safe from our guns. The swell would have prevented us from getting their bodies off the ice, should the hunt be successful.

During the day we counted eight full-grown Polar Bears, six males, two females each with two cubs. We were not able to hunt them. Two separate parties had set forth during the afternoon but owing to the loftiness of the ice upon which the bears travelled—in places twice as high from the sea as the hull of the schooner itself—those in the small dory soon lost sight of the animals high above them while we, standing on the schooner, could follow the movements of the game at all times. Also the formidable cakes, heaving up and down on the swell, rode close to one another, jamming together and closing any possible lane through which the small dory might push its way in any degree of safety. Perhaps the great creatures were laughing a little to themselves when they considered the invulnerableness of the wilderness in which they had chosen to dwell. Surrounded by Polar ice-fields, making use of ice as a solid perch on which to rest, sleep, eat, and mate, and lastly as a mighty look-out from which to detect any alien object, they had remained so far master of their fate.

These bears, *Thalarctos maritimus,* are of the same species, though of different variety, as those found near Hudson Bay, Ellesmere Land, and Spitzbergen. Yet despite this fact, like the walrus, they were of far greater size than their Atlantic cousins. Moreover, we found that they reached in some cases even greater size than the Brown Bear known as the largest carnivorous animal on earth. Perhaps this is caused by the abundance of food near the shores of this Arctic island, the carcasses of seal and walrus towed in the drift between the island and Siberia. Besides these carcasses they devour eggs, fish, shrimps, mollusks, sea weeds, foxes and when on land, the grass and roots. And like a wolf scenting a wounded deer, the White Bear can detect a possible feast at a distance of ten to twenty miles. In chase of an odorous delicacy he can swim at the rate of six miles per hour.

We soon learned also that this aquatic mammal is not so lazy as he appears to be in the Zoos. He can plunge, with a suddenness, from the lofty peak of a tower of ice into the sea below and, hadn't Big John once said, "Polar Bear kill lots Eskimo. . . ."

On the following morning when one of our hunters—supplied with the 220 grain cartridge, same as we used on the Alaska Peninsula—put out in the whaleboat, a mate at the oars, two Eskimos amidship, and the man with the rifle in the bow, we witnessed for the first time the fear of the primitive man in close quarters with his greatest enemy.

The small white boat rowed towards the iceberg-like hummock upon which stood the great white beast, sniffing the air from the topmost pinnacle. His stronghold rose and fell, and so did the boat. There was no climbing upon a nearby cake, as in the walrus hunt, because of the swell and the height of the ice above the water.

This bear was fat, and a beauty. Every move of the approaching party he watched. Quite pleased with himself, certain of his mightiness where none dare dispute him, old bruin calmly wiggled the black tip of his white nose and followed with his credulous eyes the boat coming across the open lead of water between rows of jagged white pillars.

Then he began to suspect. This something was advancing too steadily to suit the wary creature. So he decided he had better amble away, but look back now and again to make quite certain everything would continue as it should.

White King of the North

A gust of wind swept towards him. He *smelled* danger! He began to run.

The gun went off.

He dived from his icy pinnacle. Propelled himself in the direction of the enemy in the small boat that was rising and falling with the swell.

Regardless of the danger of capsizing, the Eskimos reared up in the dory. Excited! Scared! The bear was coming to attack. . . . Frightened, they called out that they wished to back away. Excited, they began to jump up and down, trying with their arms to wave off the offending, raging animal that had felt somewhere on his hide the sharp wound of a bullet.*

The scene, to watch, seemed unreal.

The white boat—a hunter now standing in the bow, rifle at his shoulder—two frightened natives —and an attacking infuriated beast.

Two more shots.

No further motion in the water. All was still.

When we hauled this superb specimen on deck we found him to measure over eleven feet in length, and a good summer skin.

*   *   *   *

Alas that I cannot describe at length our hunting for this White Bear in the Siberian Arctic be-

* John Katungazuk, whom we called Big John, lost his life, while hunting Polar Bear, during the winter of 1930-31.

cause each new hunt was as thrilling as the last one. And too we sensed always each minute, each second, that the wind might turn; that we would be forced to set sail and leave the North for that year—anyway—and maybe forever. We had, with immense difficulty, found the edge of the Polar ice-pack and accordingly stood in immediate danger of being caught.

Constantly on deck, watching the little ship plunge against ice that the bow severed in two and broke away—at the same time feeling other pans bang against the wooden hull, causing her to shiver from stem to stern—seeing men with long rods trying to push the offending humps off twin propellers, and now and then hearing orders to the engine room for full steam ahead in order to escape as immediately as possible what lay ahead —all, all, proved an experience during which our nerves were as on edge as they would be with a painfully aching tooth.

Yet despite these difficulties, during four days and three nights we cruised, all pennants flying, within the proximity of that elusive island in the Arctic ice. . . . Each one of us hoped we would not only get a chance at, but be able to bring home a white bearskin to spread out on a floor in royal luxuriance and serve during a lifetime as reminder of adventures we might never be able to equal again.

By the third day Frances, John, and Rochester had contributed their bit towards the Museum, or for themselves as the case might be. Frances had two opportunities and it was splendid to see the way she came out of the second hunt—her face wreathed in smiles as she accepted congratulations from every member of the equally pleased crew. Her bear was as large as the two specimens taken by the men. And even they were glad.

Now it had come down to Mrs. Slaughter and the writer of this tale. Would we fail? Or would we succeed? Time was speeding, ice was changing rapidly, and we would be fortunate to get one chance, certainly never two.

From here I shall quote my diary, written that very same night. . . .

"At eight o'clock we started searching the ice. The Eskimos looked tired. They had been on deck all night. Thoughtful souls—they confided that they wanted "all ladies to get Polar Bears." And then—"No Eskimo ladies like 'em Polar Bear but white ladies—they shoot good"—so in order to find us game they had not gone below for rest.

"Two bears were seen, almost at the same instant. This meant opportunity for the two of us.

She went off with her husband, one Eskimo, and second mate. I with mine, Little John and first mate. In our boat John steered, his wife sat in the bow—waiting to pull the trigger.

"Our quarry was restless before we started. By the time we managed to propel the boat between alarmingly large floes he had changed his position on his eminence of ice, and glanced down, facing us squarely. We wedged nearer. Then,—somehow I hadn't expected to reach him so soon!—he loomed close, just ahead. Head up, looking straight at us, he gave the appearance of being ready to spring. I must have gotten buck fever. Instead of acting at once I turned in my seat and called: 'Where shall I shoot?'

. . . "Imagine such a question after all the drawings of bear anatomy that I had had placed before me for study! . . .

" 'The Black spot,' floated back from the stern.

" 'What black spot?'

" 'On his chest—of course!'

"But it was terribly uncomfortable perched in the narrow bow of that small boat, and wobbly, too. My many layers of warm clothing were bulky as the rifle went up, aimed towards the black spot directly in the center of his chest.

" 'My God—shoot!' hollered a voice behind.

"Well, I did. And I missed. Completely!

"In a flash the beast catapulted from the ice,—disappearing on the opposite side. We searched for him, never knowing whether he might come up angrily near, but we did not see him again. Only water and ice and a carcass of walrus on which he had been eating. Hence the black spot.

"Finally we turned about and headed in the direction of the schooner. My disappointment, my humiliation, were indescribable. I never once looked back into the faces of the three men, behind.

"When from around the ice—as though they were rounding a building on the corner of a street, they had been so entirely cut off from our view—silently stole the other boat, carrying the other huntress, her face white and set.

"I hated to ask. Despite her face I feared she had been successful.

" 'Did you get your bear, Courtney?' She called across.

" *'No!'*

" 'Neither did I. I wounded him but we never saw him again.'

"On we paddled. My husband had not uttered a word. I couldn't stand it any longer so I heard myself say: 'John, why didn't you turn the boat more? I was in the wrong position.'

"You'll never get a better chance to kill any

bear!' was all he said. And I remembered that he had made much the same comment at some earlier time—regarding my miss of a small fast-flying bird. . . .

"I feel he might at least have said he was sorry. But even though I realize he acted this way because he wanted so terribly that I get a Polar Bear, his lack of sympathy annoys.

"Joe Slaughter has just come up while I write this. She is as glum as I am. She complains that her husband could have made things easier for her, too. Isn't it ridiculous! Neither of us have spoken to the two men since we came back to the schooner. If *Reno* had been on some cake of ice—we both would have taken up residence immediately.

"But here they come, the two men themselves, —down the steps.

"John is laughing. . . .""
The diary ends off here, abruptly.

But I can see again that scene in the warm dark-panelled main cabin as though it were yesterday. John came in laughing; the man behind him wore a broad smile.

"Little John has just taken us to task," my heretofore best friend began, "for scolding our wives. He says that King Island ladies often miss Polar Bears but they say nothing, they pay no attention, since 'they'—*just ladies!*"

Then we all burst out laughing. The tension had lifted.

Later in the privacy of our own cabin the man with me explained: "Listen, dear," he said, "I didn't mind so much your not being successful, although you certainly should have done better!—but you should have taken your miss—and bounced up with a smile. Never blame anybody else when you fail in the hunting field. . . . Everyone, you know, loves a good loser."

*   *   *   *

Cheered on by the fact that two native guides did not scorn "Ladies" for their faulty aim, two of us awoke the following day with new courage and a better knowledge of how to behave under adverse circumstances. As my husband said, that morning at the breakfast table, "we had been enjoying more experiences than most women ever have the opportunity of meeting, and we had become a trifle too cocky concerning our powers with the rifle.". . . But we were cocky no more.

Bears, luckily, were sighted again. For our especial benefit it had been decided to postpone sailing for more southerly waters until noon, though it would be taking somewhat of a chance—the barometer falling and the wind shifting southeast.

By eleven o'clock the other family had set forth once more, this time in the whaleboat. Accompanied by John, in order that he might steer the boat while the other husband gave undivided attention and instructions to his wife, they paddled away.

The rest of us watched the hunt from deck. This Diana, tempered by experience, made a clean shot and we saw her target fall, not to rise again.

Despite confidence in herself being badly shaken, there was one onlooker who anxiously awaited their return, so that she too might push off, might leave the schooner in the hunt for one more bear that was still visible on a not too distant floe. But on glancing at the ship's clock above the wheel room, it told her that the chances were growing slim—since the hour was now 11:30 and the orders had been to sail not later than noon.

"Madam, there's a bear!" The steward yelled out. "See—it's swimming out there. . . . Quick. . . . Where's your gun?"

A sailor lamented with a shout that the bear was getting away too fast, would disappear in the high hummocks of ice before the launch might be lowered. The bear was heading towards the stern.

Rifle, and ammunition, were already on deck. It did not take long to find them. . . .

He was lovely, that swimming creature with his white ears standing up like those of a chow dog.

And he was more beautiful still when he lay on deck—waiting to surprise the unsuspecting party in the whaleboat on their return—my bear.

Luncheon, that day, proved to be an infinitely gayer affair than supper of the preceding night.

LATE SUMMER

IX

Quest of the Steelhead
WHEN UP AGAINST THE ROGUE

WHAT IS HE . . . SALMON OR TROUT? He appears
to possess a dual personality. *Salmo gairdneri* is
his name. An authority explains him thus: "A
large sea-trout growing to weight of twenty pounds
or more, is migratory like the salmon, ascending
rivers to spawn many hundreds of miles. . . ."
The description goes on to list the Pacific States
in which this "salmon trout" is taken as he battles
his way upstream to spawn in the early spring. But
the statement does not say, to appease a rather
morbid curiosity, whether the old one dies or lives
on, when creation is complete. . . . "They are
found in the lower parts of rivers in a spent condition when the usual spring run of the salmon commences." It makes no difference to this story
whether death comes to him, after creation, as it
does to the Pacific salmon, except that the steelhead, like the other game fighter, has captured my
imagination. It has managed to intrigue me, and
has thrust itself—as will be seen later—into a niche
of our lives.

Fishermen may tell you there are steelhead in

streams of the Middle West. Perhaps there are. But, you will decide by the tone of voice in which they speak, that these are not *the* steelhead. They are not the *Steelhead* of the Rogue.

The difference we had to discover for ourselves.

Off we went to the West Coast, our transcontinental stateroom cluttered with the usual fly-fishing retinue—objects stowed on the rack, on the sofa, and tin boxes stuffed into corners. Why is it a person can find so much to laugh at in the outfit for the sport of angling? Possibly it is because the greatest part of it is so small, almost dinky, so bothering to keep track of in the house, and so hard to handle with ten clumsy fingers. "Women ought to be able to tie on a fly much easier than men do," a friend once said when he watched my fingers turn into thumbs as they worked with an aggravatingly tiny leader and fly. "Why?". . . "Oh—because you have to thread so many needles."

Outfit for any sport can be absurd. The golf ball is silliest when you analyze it. And what about riding to hounds—all dressed up in smart boots and pink coat, when an old sweater, any pair of trousers, puttees, shoes, and the horse bare-of-back, could serve equally as well, if you could sit your mount well enough. But no, we have special saddles fashioned to fit; we *oh* and *ah* over bridles, or tack as I should say. Magazines and books are published on the subject. So it is with bird shooting and big-game hunting. Why not any gun and any shell? Thus, when realizing that after writing all these stories of birds and game I have not once mentioned how truly funny the racket of firearms and ammunition and gunning can seem, I decide I was dull to have taken it all so seriously. For I did mean to laugh at it more, since it can produce many chuckles, outwardly and inwardly, when the struggle is over and only memories remain. But there is a reason why I wrote so solemnly. Because—when the impact of each new experience was actually taking place—it *was* serious! Terribly so. Grimly serious.

Though I may laugh now at our quest of the awe-inspiring steelhead . . . I did not laugh then.

*   *   *   *

It was September. We were not far from the town of Medford, Oregon. Mountains, fertile valleys, orchards with their thousands of fruit trees stretched before us as far as we could see. Through the open window of the motor we caught the rich odor of ripe red apples while we sped onward towards the River Rogue.

"Think Barnes' Riffle the best bet today," our host sang out from his seat behind the wheel.

When he spoke I happened to be glancing down

169

at a pair of enormous boots, with hob-nails on their soles, which were purchased that morning on our arrival in Medford, and now enclosed feet that were strangely mine, feet that I never dreamed could appear so huge and so ugly. They were not, could not be the belongings of a "lady." The salesman had exclaimed, "Sure you need 'em! . . . Plenty of wool socks to make 'em comfy! . . . You need 'em to hold you down if for nothing else. I guess you folks from the East don't know the Rogue until you've stepped into her. Then"—and his thin tight-skinned face burst into a smile—"Oh Boy!"

"Yeah . . . Barnes' a good bet," the man beside the driver agreed. "Bill caught his there yesterday."

"How do you mean *his?*" I hazarded.

"His steelhead," some one explained and then laughed when he saw my expression.

Did sportsmen actually boast of one fish? Could this be? Why all this dither about steelhead? Had we travelled thousands of miles to be contented over the catching of one fish a day? If so, let's go back to the trout streams where even a no-good fisherwoman might land a few, though barely keepers. . . . A steelhead! Would I get one?

We were four in that car, three ardent fishermen and one wife. Slater, our host, had been fishing the Rogue off and on ever since the opening of the season. He had invited the two of us, and Harry—to visit him in his bachelor's lodge from where we had just emerged to go forth in search of steelhead.

Beyond, the Rogue now glistened. We could hear its rumble, its loud plashing as it tumbled over huge boulders and cascaded in a mad rush towards the sea.

"She's some baby—that river!" Harry murmured respectfully as he pulled forth a cigarette, his last until lunch, and lit it. His voice held concealed laughter, concealed amusement perhaps at the anticipation of events which might follow.

We had stopped the car in a grove of willows. Close ahead roared the Rogue. Like a race-horse dashing to the finish line, this river had let out all its strength and on it galloped. The clerk had been justified, then, when he told me: "You need 'em to hold you down. . . ." How could any one stand against the onslaught of that live thing which I saw beyond the trees? . . . This was no peaceful winding stream.

"Here's your rod." John said, handing me a five-ounce Leonard. He himself would use a six-ounce rod of the same make. Harry's was also a Leonard, of five and a half ounces, and I cannot remember the fourth. Heatedly, we discussed the enigma of flies as we put together our rods. The selection would be, as usual, as vital to success as the performance of a hunting dog in the game bird field.

"Do you think you can change it—when in the river?" Slater inquired, referring to my fly with a meaningful grin as he came forward to escort me to the water's edge. I could not answer, only grinned in return. A gay selection of feathers were tucked nicely in a small round aluminum box over my chest—in one of the many mysterious pockets of a fishing-jacket. Could I get at it, open it, choose one, put it back, remove the old one, tie on a new selection—when in the river?

"Well, let's go!" Harry cried with the restless enthusiasm of the captain of a Harvard football team, ready for the match with Yale to commence. "What's the delay?" Then he surged ahead and grabbed my arm. "Come with me. . . . I'll put you out there in a pool where you're bound to get a strike." Being the only feminine member of our party of four was very pleasant. I couldn't help but receive plenty of courteous attention.

The whirling waters licked higher. A cold clammy sensation rose up along the legs, the knees, the thighs, the waist. No more could we hear the cheery twittering of birds. We heard only the Rogue, and saw deep shadows reaching out over the river from the shore, making pools loom deep and black and uninviting, suggestive of unattractive depths.

Beneath the heavy hob-nailed boots we felt jagged boulders, over which we stepped, pushing against the current. Some, rough and irregular, others were flat and slippery. One foot heading the procession, warning the other, shoved forth searchingly, like the feeler of an insect, then on they both advanced. It was quite awful—the departure from the last firm rock encountered. Awful because of a moment when nothing but swirling depths seemed to yawn beneath. And the Rogue seemed to possess a fund of lore, of tales concerning the luckless ones who had lost their balance and gone bobbing down into the white-crested whirlpools like a bundle of old rags.

"Now throw out your line," Harry was directing. "Get out a long line—long as you possibly can. Then quarter your water and don't miss any. It's *good* right over there!"

Having announced this, he went away and left me, the noisy river pounding in my ears. The two others had long since disappeared, either down stream and round the bend, or else along the bank until they should reach a likely-looking riffle where the grandfather fish would be waiting, and then —out they would push into the current.

What were my feelings—there alone—legs not feeling quite sure of their strength? The emotion that sang to the tune of water surging over boulders was not nameless—like the quiet emotion felt while wading a trout stream—it was fear, fear of the dangerous swiftness as I stood there alone, not daring to proceed downstream. For this was stronger liquor, heady liquor, that made your head spin and your feet feel like a part of some one else.

No guide to make suggestions. No one on whom to depend.

Standing a little to one side gave a person added balance, and a little more purchase with the shoes. But I felt sure it might be but a matter of time until something wrong would occur. . . . To start with—one cast shoreward and a tree or snag could incapacitate my line, and leader. No one could retrieve the fastened fly.

However, not long afterward one more fisherman forgot the swiftness of the current, and the blackness ·of the depths beneath the surface, as she commenced to toss out, and bring back the fly with all the zeal that she could muster. It *must* attract a steelhead.

Hours passed. Literally hours! A slight breeze sprung up and ruffled the fragile green plumes of willows. The odor of clean earthy things, and tall trees and apples in crates drifted out on that breeze. And slowly down the river this fisher-woman went. But there was one thing she could not do—change her fly. The current was too engrossing.

Each cast she felt hopeful as she quartered the likely-looking water in much the same way as a good grouse dog quarters his ground. Each new riffle looked inviting to steelhead. Each stumble made her a trifle less sure-footed than before.

What time could it be? Late. Long after a respectable luncheon hour. And no human being in sight. No traffic on the Rogue that day.

Were the three men having luck? At least their flies would be causing no splash, and they were perhaps changing the lures a dozen times.

"Catch anything?" a voice shouted from some-where behind.

It was our host, himself, navigating downstream with no little difficulty.

"No," I answered. "Did you?"

"Skunked!" he cried with a laugh in his voice, and adding "Let's eat, anyhow, I'm starved." He waded nearer. "Wait until I get Harry! . . . Just wait! . . ." He was laughing aloud.

"Why?"

"He inveigled me out to where he said Freddie Atkins had caught a big one earlier this morning—

and then roared with laughter when I stepped in up to my neck."

A few minutes later, with his assistance, we were back on firm ground. And were soon attacking with relish the lunch of cold chicken, sandwiches and fruit that the Chinaman had prepared. On the verge of making-away with more than our share the two other fishermen made a wet and discouraged appearance.

Despite their decidedly tell-tale faces we decided to shout, "Get anything?"

"Skunked!" came one more reply.

They dropped onto the ground near us. "Blast it!" grumbled Harry as he reached for the leg of a chicken, "Not a *damn* thing even smelled my fly. Pardon my French. . . . I'm going to stick to my own hunch next time. It's too bright for a *Dusty Miller.*"

We laughed. The expression of his face was that of a small boy half angry and half sorry for himself.

Nothing daunted, fifteen minutes later saw us at it again. Once more we separated and chose our own riffles. The afternoon sun commenced to play longer patterns over the darkening river, and then dropped out of sight behind the mountains.

Still I cast.

Evening came. The earthy fragrance lost its

sweetness, became strong, and bitter. The water, beating against waders, became colder and less inviting.

It was then that voices floated above the tumult of the Rogue: voices arguing about flies and riffles. Voices that brought no tidings of success.

*   *   *   *

The second day bigger things happened. We were fishing a more humanly populated bend of the Rogue. Here, like in all trout streams, we met friendly, chatty strangers who told their own tales of good or bad luck, and offered advice. Harry, though having vowed the day before that he would "stick to his own hunch next time," took the suggestion of the best-known fisherman on the stream, Freddie Atkins, we will call him, and tied on a fly he had never tried before. I had caught up with Harry where he stood on a gravel spit, smiling to himself as he slipped the final knot.

"We'll show them!" he chuckled, and back he stepped into the river. Far out he headed towards a deep hole where the waves licked close to the top of his waders. "Be sure you don't let water get down inside your waders. . . . Or they'll fill up and you'll sink," he had explained that very morning when we were still motoring towards our destination.

177

Suddenly I saw his right wrist give a violent jerk—the automatic reel a click. *Bzzz*—it was commencing to run out. Downstream from the fisherman, a large silvery fish had struck and broke water.

The man lunged ahead, holding his rod firmly up, resisting the pull of his quarry. No slack line. Faster the reel unwound. The game fish commenced his fight for freedom.

Here was no *fontinalis*, no under-water fighter. Having risen for artificial feathers this finned acrobat continued to leap repeatedly out of the water, each time a shower of white crystals pouring off his long shining body. Then down he would flop, wildly tearing to right, and left, cutting the water in a wide angry swirl.

The fish had become frantic. The reel had nearly run out. In between his furious spurts downstream, enraged at his apparent impotence in not being able to rip free, the large steelhead persisted in the wild aerial flights which he must have known would eventually destroy his strength.

As for the man, he stumbled on. Grey felt hat shoved to the rear of his baldish head gave the bright sunlight a chance to reveal beads of perspiration standing across his forehead.

He was laughing. . . . "Some Babies!" he shouted to me on shore from where I followed the struggle between man and the courageous fish.

And as he spoke, even before the words had tossed from his lips, the fish gave a fresh plunge downstream. Once more the reel whizzed. . . . Then, for no reason, it stopped. Stopped altogether. An ominous silence . . . a silence pregnant with the sound of the Rogue.

"Whew!" grunted the man, taking time out to find his handkerchief and mop his face. "It's a big one! . . . There it goes——"

Again the glistening body tossed itself out of the churning water, darting through the air, and down. Again it swooped to right, and left.

Minute after minute ticked by. This was a struggle for existence to be admired.

The fisherman, with the steelhead on the end of his line, commenced to back up towards the narrow reef of gravel lying close to shore. He was slowly reeling in.

"Want to take the rod—and feel him?" he shouted. "He's a good five pounder."

"No—it might still get away. Thank you."

"Not this one!" his proud voice came back minutes later as he leaned over and removed the hook.

Spurred on by this exciting drama the afternoon assumed fresh importance. But Harry was the only one in our party who tasted success.

The morning of the third day the other member of our family had luck, and landed a four pounder.

"Look here," he said, in a husbandly manner, when we met at noon, "Give me your rod. *You* will never catch anything—with a fly!"

We stepped out on to shore. I gave him the rod.

"I'm going to put on a spinner."

He opened a case, fingered a small silvery-gold object, took it out, his fingers intent on their task.

"There!" he explained shortly and glanced up with a twinkle in his eye. "If you catch anything—unless you want to you needn't admit the spinner—unless some one asks. . . ."

Thus prepared, my line bedecked with a dazzling lure, and having been divulged the secret lair where a large fish had been seen and not caught, I thanked him and hurried away to the business of attracting it to my line. That afternoon would be our last on the Rogue. And once more the element of time pressed close. I could not, after travelling all this way to the West Coast, return without one steelhead.

Possibly the spinner, combined with the almost frantic desire to hasten on coveted success, gave me added nerve. Whatever it was, the large shoes shoved off in the direction of a deeper pool than they had heretofore dared to enter, the pool just above the riffle where the big fish had been known to lie.

The surging water climbed high, rippling to the top of waist-high waders. Balancing precariously on a slippery rock, I threw out the shiny bait, trying to make as little splash as possible. It glittered for a moment in the afternoon sun, then settled into the alluring pool.

The terrific pressure of the river, at that spot, was a handicap. It was almost essential to pay more attention to balance than to the riffle I had begun to cover. With the wind behind, the line had begun to go out nicely—when . . . Wham! . . . Something entirely unexpected struck me from behind. It came again. Nearly knocked me over as though I had been a pin in a bowling alley. Sickening shivers! All in a flash I thought first of snakes. . . . Then of the luckless ones who had been sucked into whirlpools. The muscles in my knees had commenced to shake, uncontrollably.

I stood there, petrified. But for fully two seconds nothing more bore down upon me from the spectral watery depths. Whatever it was, the lump had swirled off downstream.

I simply had to get a steelhead! A little thing like a dead body should not put me out of the running. Every one else now had one, all except Slater who lived there all summer and, undoubtedly, was being a proper host, taking the poorest locations for himself.

So on pushed the shoes, seeking another rock, and even a more tempting pool than the one just tried.

Time passed. Nothing even bothered to notice the beautiful spinner. Would anything ever— Whang!—and then another tug. . . . Something huge! The rod nearly flew out of my hand. The tip all but split in two. I could scarcely hold it. The fish was running. . . . What should I do? . . . I'd give it line . . . more line. It was running faster. . . . Suddenly it heaved itself out of the water. And all those shiny crystals dripped off of it. . . . Then down. . . . Then up. . . . I wished Harry were there to help. . . . Lucky for me it was well out in the middle of the river.

Must give it more line. . . . The reel was tearing out, unwinding so fast it hurt my hand. . . . A Steelhead! . . . Mustn't lose it. . . . I had to follow it downstream. . . . Nothing else to be done. . . . Whoop! . . . Out again of the water. . . .

I was so excited I was like a crazy person. Was it time yet to reel in? No, not yet. On we plunged, the fish and I, downstream.

In a flash everything went black. I had stepped

off a rock into a bottomless abyss. I absolutely must catch on to something before—But I mustn't lose that fish!——

I was floating. . . . Must catch on to something! Down into the water went the left arm. This nearly turned me over entirely. The current seemed more powerful than ever. Even the enormous shoes weren't holding me down. They were rising . . . rising upwards and out. . . . I went on floating. . . . Could I keep my head out of water?

Cold waves trickled inside the belted waders. I was now in the sitting position of a person in an unstable swing, only with nothing beneath on which to sit. The big shoes had entirely lost their efficacious powers. They were merely floating ahead of me.

Years took place in those gruesome seconds. It was only a matter of time until I might go down for good——

But no—a boulder was swimming towards me. It bumped against the shoes. Bumped hard—and hurt. Then I found myself clinging to it, hysterically. It was a wonderful boulder, it had probably saved my life. . . .

For a second I couldn't even think, had only just begun to breathe normally.

"Hello there!" shouted a voice. . . . Where

was that voice? In some other world, some other consciousness?

"What are you doing out there? Come back at once!"

"I can't," I called feebly. "Come out and get me."

A splashing from near shore. Some one coming to get me. . . .

And then I remembered! It all came back to me. . . . I had had a steelhead on my line . . . had almost caught it . . . when——

"You'll get in trouble out in that deep water!" a voice chided as John waded over and grabbed me by the arm.

"But I had a steelhead——"

"Hurry up—and come in where it's shallow."

*   *   *   *

Being taken by the arm was very pleasant. We passed by a green pool close to the bank where dying salmon—large, Pacific salmon that had lost their brilliant silver coloring and were greenish and mouldy looking—twisted this way and that. Their fins along their backs protruded out of the water as they rolled from one side to the other, apparently oblivious of anything but the deep sand in which they were preparing to hollow out their graves.

Quest of the Steelhead

"Different than they were in British Columbia where we caught them, aren't they? . . . This is their birth stream where they've come home to die," John was saying.

So that was what had hit me in the back, a half-dead salmon! . . . One of those poor helpless creatures. I forgave the salmon, but I couldn't forgive the Rogue—well-named river—for depriving me of my strike.

X

Three Big Rainbows

PERHAPS I AM LEAVING A WRONG IMPRESSION. The impression that life, for us, has been one continual merry-go-round of sport—one continual search for this recreation and that adventure. Quite the contrary. These excursions into the refreshing peace of woods and waters have been our greatest luxuries. And now, since for several years I have been a partner who went and enjoyed, wept and laughed, and every so often succeeded, I have come to understand why:—"Today large numbers of men overwork for eleven months of the year in order to be able to hunt or fish during the twelfth." These true words of Haldane's were found in a recent *Harpers* paper called "In Defense of Luxury."

A man who loves his guns and tackle, feels within him at every new season of the year the urge to put them to use, to get away somewhere—somewhere that cannot be penetrated by telephones, and business deals, and bills, and worries. Especially during these last three years. So it has been with us. In my notes I remarked, "The deeper became the depression the more we trout-fished on Sundays." The more tired we were, or worried, and when things seemed to pile too high, we sneaked off to the sanctuary of the woods for a week-end that we knew, no matter how brief, would send us back to the battlefield invigorated in body, and our thoughts put in order.

Grouse shooting during ten days in October, only occasional duck shooting when we had no camp, trout fishing each spring and summer, a day here and there on the snipe marsh, and at last quail shooting, the best of all—have been our short and recent retreats, our closed door against any interruptions.

"So long as we retain fish in our streams and wild game in our fields and forests, our civilization is safe," is a quoted saying from the introduction to that delightful book *The Dumbbell of Brookfield*. When I read it, for the first time, I thought it rang fair enough. But now I know its full significance. For I have seen and talked with unemployed men—unfortunate products of our machine civilization—their wives and children, who have sought during the past three summers the beautiful streams of Wisconsin and Michigan on the banks of which they have made camps and there lived happily for two and three months at a time. The father, his heart still in the cities where he hoped a job might soon be waiting, would periodically jump into his truck and "beat it," as one expressed himself, "back to the city to see what might be open," only to return and forget his fresh disappointment in the joyful casting of a fly.

Any man who has talked with these outdoor-minded husbands, and their wives, and caught a cheerful philosophy in the face of adversity, mingled with a sort of fierce pride in this great country itself, has found an experience in human values and courage, and faith that all will go well in the end. It is a lesson in fellowship of human kind, as well. For the democracy of the fishing stream brings humble contacts that make of life a richer experience.

Three successive seasons of trout fishing not far from home—for brook, German brown or rainbow —have not as yet offered "Marvelous fishing!" though we have found "Good fishing!" The reason being:—we have not fished privately stocked streams or rivers, ponds or lakes. The streams we waded, with one exception, have been open to the public from their source to where they emptied into some lake, or gulf, and here we have met the humble individuals of whom I speak. The Big Manistee River—so far the best—the Pine, the Au Sable, well known for German browns, the Pere Marquette and the Black River reputed to be alive with brook trout, yet yielded little on the warm sunny day we were there, are all quite worth the trip if you don't mind occasional disappointing days. These are streams in the lower Peninsula of Michigan, famed for trout. The Little Muskegon River gave us a good afternoon of small-mouth bass fishing with trout rods and bass fly.

One down-and-outer who was bolstering up his spirits, and those of his wife and two young sons, by spending the summer on the Manistee, began telling me of the Neversink. He was, incidentally, the most beautiful dry fly artist it had ever been my privilege to watch in action. And he had not always been in the dejected condition he was, the times had made him so. In New York he had once had a good job.

"That is a wonderful piece of water, isn't it?" I had said, referring to the river in New York State.

"It's a rich man's stream, the Neversink, I'm tellin' you! A poor man like I am has no business fishin' it. It's all posted—clear down—on both sides. You can't get in except at bridges—and you can't get out except at bridges. And them bridges is mighty few and far between when a fellow's ready to quit. But it's lousy with fish."

A day or so before, on a well-known creek whose name I choose to forget, I had come across the same situation. Some game hog had stretched a wire fence along both banks, and thrown heavy logs in the stream itself so wading was well-nigh impossible, because of the deep holes formed by these logs. He was guarding all the water, as far down as his land went, for his own use in a boat. And I had compared him at the time to a man who happened to own land on two sides of a public highway and as a result had cut bumps and ridges into the concrete road so no car would care to pass.

Therefore, I well understood this poor man's disgust at being kept out of water which was "lousy with fish" when the stream itself rightfully belonged to all. In following the sport of fishing, open to any man who can afford a rod, old clothes and a license, a person cannot help but better comprehend the meaning of democracy, privilege for the masses. For this is their recreation. They cannot belong to golf clubs, and enjoy the society sports of polo, and fox hunting, even golf.

"But, Madam," he now said very politely as he, an American citizen, was of English birth, "I can show you where there's a very big rainbow. I've raised him twice this summer and he's broken my tackle—every time."

This was a fish! Who wouldn't hearken to such an invitation?

He took me with him. It was a lovely day in early September, the day preceding Labor Day. It was a well-known fact that the season was too well advanced for brook in any great numbers to rise to a fly, therefore large rainbow were now the target of most fishermen. These big boys had returned to the smaller rivers after having travelled probably hundreds of miles to seek the Great Lakes, or I don't know where, during July and August. They, like the steelhead in the Rogue, and the Pacific salmon in the rivers of the West Coast, had come back to their home stream to spawn.

"You've got somethin', I'm tellin' you, if you've got a five-pound rainbow on one of them four-ounce rods!" He was anticipating aloud as he examined my new little Thomas.

"What will I use?" I asked.

"Dry fly, of course!" he answered. "I would never use anything else. Wet fly is not much better than plunking." (He had used this verb once before in reference to his wife. She was a "plunker." Whether she caught fish or not—seeing she refused to learn how to use a fly—was not the point. He would never give her any credit. She would always be just a plain "plunker.")

"What kind?"

"I prefer grey hackle, myself. Best fly of all of 'em. I tie my own. Just finished tyin' a new bunch up there now," pointing to the camp on the high bluff. "Plymouth Rock rooster, I use."

A few minutes later he had shown me the pool, under a long grey log that jutted out from shore. And we wasted no further time. "He's in there as sure as I'm standin' in this stream. I raised him just yesterday," the man's voice came from behind me.

Never have I cast better. Each instant was vibrant with the expectancy that the big boy would rise to my lure, a grey hackle. But instead, an eleven-inch *fontinalis* leaped at it almost at once. Even a speckled trout of eleven inches, usually very acceptable, this day of big hopes seemed scarcely more than a keeper. I didn't want it. Ironically, I couldn't lose it no matter how much I hoped to. The fight it put up was spoiling the water. The small pool was now thoroughly threshed out for several hours at least. Such was our luck.

That night, back at the club, we listened to famous Labor Day catches of other years. The morrow would be the closing day of this season. Would Labor Day fail us? On the September holiday in 1931, on the Big Manistee River near Grayling, Mr. Fred N. Rowe was using, at the same time, tied one considerably above the other, two number twelve Cahill wet flies. He was letting them sink a little after he had dropped them gently into a likely hole, when, with one cast, at the same instant, he hooked a twenty-inch rainbow on the upper fly, and with the lower, a seventeen-inch fellow of the same species. What is more, he landed them both. I know Mr. Rowe and believe in his honesty. Also, he had two witnesses.

Here is another Labor Day catch equally as honest. Mr. A. Dexter Swain, Jr., whose father was that night a guest at our club and who told this story, took with him to the Little Manistee a friend who had never fly-fished, but who had, actually, spent a few conscientious hours of preparation in his back yard for this particular trip. He could cast, but was feeling rather timid.

On his second cast, in a hole to where he had been guided, an enormous rainbow struck at his artificial lure. And in due time, a half hour or so, he brought him in,—a twenty-four and a half inch gentleman who weighed four pounds dressed.

Such was the success of others. We could all scarcely wait, after this conversation that had whetted our appetites for bigger and better fish, until the night passed and day dawned. While we were brushing up the hearth before retiring and tidying wet waders and boots before the open fireplace, a distinguished sportsman and gentleman from New York—a man who had come West each August for ten or fifteen years to get a mess of brook, and, always, hoping to get *one* record rainbow, which he usually did—invited us to stop what we were doing and listen for a moment to him. "You know perfectly well," he announced, "and there's no use fooling yourself—that the only *sure way* to catch big rainbows this time of year is by minnows! You might get an occasional one to rise for a fly, but certainly not very often." And he was a fine fly fisherman, we all knew.

This I did not forget the next morning when we were making ready to start. "Ben," I whispered, "will you get me some minnows?" Ben was the guide and caretaker. "Minnies?—Sure!" he laughed. "And I bet you catch a big one. Big rainbows always feed on them big minnies."

Big rainbows were indeed intriguing creatures. Once they returned to the river they never moved, it seemed, from their holes. There were never two of them, either, in one hole. Never, so far as any of the ten or twelve experienced stream fishermen, and fellow club members, knew about. Each big boy had his own lair. There he crouched, in hiding. "Wherever you see a kind of baye (meaning bayou) and then a deep black hole you're almost sure to find a big rainbow," Ben explained. "The minnies stay in that shallow baye and the big trout lay there close to pounce on 'em. They won't go so very fur to find their food." These large exciting fish, kings of their castles and lords of all they surveyed, reminded me of the huge male Alaskan Brown Bear. This independent four-legged creature usually takes unto himself a mountain side and there fends off all marauders. "Where do the mates of these big rainbow keep themselves?" I inquired of Ben. "In one hole—aren't there *ever* two?" Ben's grey eyes broke into a twinkle. "I never did know about that," he said.

We were off. No brook trout today. No German browns. Nothing but one big grandfather rainbow apiece. Our particular party consisted of John, Ben, and myself. We parked the car fairly conveniently near three different, and equally promising holes. We were to go our own separate ways, and meet again in an hour and a half. We were not unlike three small boys bound for their favorite fishing hole. And it was then I recalled a saying of Samuel Johnson's: "A fishing rod is a stick with a hook at one end and a fool at the other."

John bent on a spent wing Royal Coachman, number ten. Ben was to try a wet Cahill, using Mr. Rowe's experience as his guide. And I, brazenly, a minnow, with an extra heavy Hewlitt leader which in comparison to our usual leaders resembled a piano wire. Also, instead of our lightest rods, we carried two five-ounce rods, and one of five and a half ounces. We were equipped for a catch of weight and size.

I stepped into the Manistee. The water was cold and swift this morning. Ahead of me, near the opposite bank, rose an old dam. Swirling black waters flowed by it. On beyond opened a mysterious bayou where minnows apparently swam about in large schools.

It all didn't take but the flash of an eye to happen.

I threw in the live minnow, watched it swim on down beyond the old rotting piles. Nothing—I tried again. This time tossed the minnow a few yards further out, let it drift down in the black gurgling water, still closer to the upright logs. Suddenly out darted a silver streak, a round fat streak that resembled, in the quick flash, a six or seven pound Pacific salmon in size and shape. With one hungry snap it grabbed my minnow. It was, they tell me, turning the small fish round in its mouth. Making up its mind as to its next move.

Then—quiet. Had it gone? I hadn't seen the streak dart back into the black hollow between the logs. I dared not even breathe, much less move a muscle below the surface of the dark swirling water. *Zowie!* It had struck again. And this time with a fierce pull as though this minnow were the only minnow it had ever seen—or would ever see.

For a moment I couldn't budge the dead weight, yet thought the next thing to do would be to direct him towards the center of the stream, away from logs round which the smart creature would most certainly wind itself and eventually tear free. I gave it the whole bend and give of my rod, but no slack. Fortunately! Because it commenced to fight with the strength of a large dog yanking at the end of a rope, trying to tear the rope out of my hold. It was exactly that sort of feeling, as though the fish were tossing its head like an angry dog in its mad effort to wrench free. Then came one enormous jerk. . . .

In another instant the silver streak flashed upward, struck out towards the black logs and to my utter astonishment, he was gone. He had been well hooked, very evidently. But now, not only was my minnow gone, but hook, and all of the leader. The piano wire leader, the strongest leader made for a trout rod. It had snapped in two. Nothing left but a helpless line floating out from the tip of my rod.

He was the biggest rainbow I had ever seen, even in pictures.

Returning to the car, feeling not as beaten as resentful of all leaders and bemoaning the fact that we were not equipped—seeing that before leaving home we had made up our minds it must be big rainbows or nothing!—with our salmon outfits, heavier lines, leaders, and hooks. . . .

Possibly the others were faring better? I hoped so.

John was there by the car, seated on the running board, holding his head, and lost in memories, or hopes, or something.

"Did you get a big one?" I called hopefully.

He looked up. He shook his head. "I had a beauty!" he explained, "A three or four pound rainbow. At least I think he was a rainbow."

"What happened?"

"He took my fly and leader and all." And in a minute, his voice rather tired, "I've waited just three years to catch a big rainbow—and then when I get one—the damn leader was no good! Had him on a dry fly, too. I don't know when I was ever so mad! . . ."

Ben was now appearing. And believe it or not he, too, had *lost* a big rainbow! His casualty was caused by the fish darting under a log in the bottom of a hole at least twenty feet deep. But Ben, lucky man, had had a few minutes of play before the drastic end occurred.

"Well, at least you folks now are sure them stories of big fish breaking up everybodies tackle

—can be true," Ben offered philosophically, as we drove off to fresh territory. "Just think how it 'ud be now if them three rainbow were in the creel! . . . Why they'd be too large to get into them baskets. We'd have to git a heavy rope."

An hour or so later as we sat under a tall Norway pine and munched on dry sandwiches—we had forgotten our thermos of hot coffee which fact added to the hard breaks of the day—our fisherman friend of the day before came by. He had been looking for us. "Madam," he said, "did you go back for that big fish where you got the eleven inch brook yesterday?"

Then we began. Three tales of woe.

The English-born fisherman, taught when a young man to cast for the rising trout, listened to them all. Then he smiled. He didn't laugh as he should have done. Fishing, in his opinion, was serious business.

"That's the luck and fun o' fishin'," he tossed back over his shoulder as he climbed back onto the driver's seat of his truck in which he, his wife and boys, were going berry picking. "Better luck— next time!" and away they went.

Of our three experiences, sad as they each were, only the story told by the one who used the dry fly had attracted this man's real interest and respect. As for me, with the minnow, it would not have meant anything to him, if I *had* landed the huge rainbow. For "wives are plunkers," is all he would have said to himself, and at the same time felt a little more certain he understood all women.

Well, I now have a great respect for the rainbow! My only regret being that I wish I could look back and think of myself, with infinite skill and gentleness, having enticed the great salmon-like fish on to a dry fly. Why hadn't it happened the day before, the afternoon when the speckled trout grabbed my grey hackle, staged a fight and spoiled the hole? It was hardly fair, luring that game silvery streak from his black lair by the sight of live meat.

This, then, is the difference between plain angling—and art. I am glad to have grown up enough to understand.

That evening the gentleman from New York wanted repeated all over again the three major tragedies. When he had heard them he gave a hearty laugh.

"I have never fished for trout with a woman," he said, after a minute. "What I would like to know is—does a sportswoman swear—when she is alone?"

WINTER

XI

Quail at "Glenwild"

Seldom do we go duck shooting any more, not, anyway, when *Glenwild* is our home. For here at our own front door, in the fields beyond our house, lie the prettiest, the gamest, and the most respected of all hunted birds, the Bob White quail.

Glenwild in the deep south of Mississippi is a cotton plantation and a quail preserve as well, where cotton and quail supplement one another in the necessary balance of existence—economic need and the pleasure of living. There are also to be had squirrels and rabbits and dove, game we do not take. Here we have come from the North to live quietly and calmly and appreciate the richness of each day as it moves inevitably from sun-up to sun-down, in a leisurely fashion so easy to enjoy. At night the balmy southern skies glistening with shining constellations each laid like crystals on a piece of fine jewelry are like clear tropic heavens seen from the helm of a ship. Only in this Southland of the United States there comes to you at dusk the faint unmistakable odor of pine—burning pine logs on some distant cabin hearth, now and then mingled with the green stronger fragrance

of tall pines still standing in the rolling woodlands.

In a way it all started on the plantation. It was
ours to love. But we never considered making it
a home. The place was merely to stop in while
shooting. Those were the days when I was audience, or a stay-at-home relegated to the brick gal-
leries and the courtyard, to the tennis courts, or
perhaps left with the colored boys who held the
horses. Only the men went quail shooting. Yet in
those days, not knowing what I was missing, like
a child I was satisfied with little.

Now there are two of us who consider it worth
while—since we can't live in two places and the
season on quail comes at the same time as the season for residing in cities—two of us who consider
it worth while giving up the attractive and stimu-
lating amusements of a sophisticated urban existence in order to dwell in the depths of the country. Thus it is each winter that we are living on
this tract of land in the deep South, and in adding
to its interests are concentrating on encouraging the
growth of wild life which to us particularly means
the raising and propagating by natural methods,
the Bob White* quail. It is indeed a fascinating
process well worth all efforts. It has far and away
increased the number of coveys on our preserve,

* See Appendix.

has eliminated the necessity and expense each year of turning out birds to live or die, and has not in any way decreased the yield of our crops. But this is something, that to go into here, would take a whole other volume in itself, of such is its importance!

This plantation has offered, as well as sport, a refuge of peace and rest from the industrial cities of the North during the last winter or two of hard times. Here, all winter I have stayed, and the children with me. Here on Saturdays—ofttimes Fridays—came the Head of the House, or in this case the Master of the Plantation, from his affairs in the North. Here has been for our guests a temporary release from all worries until the dreaded Sunday night that comes all too soon.

So, thankful I was when we actually changed our winter residence from a great Northern city that we all loved, to a plantation in the South, that at last I was no longer considered only an onlooker at a man's sport. At last it had become a recognized part of my own life. Dogs, and guns, and hunting togs had already replaced fur coats and were becoming more important than a closet full of dressed-up clothes. "Mother has gone hunting," my children now smile and say to any casual visitor who might be calling, and to them it seems little different than as though they had said, "Mother is planting tulips."

It was Mac, Pal, Girlie and the others who aided a former city dweller in finding a substitute for lectures, and museums, concerts, theaters, clubs, movies and shops, all the engrossing panorama of things and people which I had once deemed essential to the joy of living. Mac, Pal, and Girlie, the grouse dog Duke, honest slow old Jake, Major and Peggy, have provided a fund of faithful friendships, a sportsmanship and companionship such as can be offered a human being by only a hunting dog. They have superseded my one-time passion for china and glass, old furniture, old silver, and new possessions. They are worth being interested in. They pay dividends in labor and affection.

Thus it is that I work hard at writing or domestic responsibilities on certain days of the week in order that I can deserve to go afield with those dogs for a part of two days, or the whole of one day, during the beginning of each week of November, December, and January. For weekends are given over to entertaining friends.

Ill with influenza during the planning of this book, the doctor who came out to call began telling me of the hard cases he had had of late, and the tremendous amount of charity he and his associates had been called upon to do among the "poor whites." He did look tired. Then he crossed his knees, pushed himself farther back in the chair, when a smile broke over his face. "But I'll work all night, every night, if necessary," he added, "so long as I can get off every now and then—with my dogs. . . . Quail shooting is the greatest pleasure in my life."

Then he glanced towards me. But I had said nothing. "Duck shooting—that's fun too. . . . But quail shooting is another matter. Quail fly fast—that's all! And, oh boy, the thrill I get when the birds go—*Burr rr.*"

*   *   *   *

Our own kennel, neither large nor small, has served satisfactorily ourselves and guests. The dogs have come from various parts of the United States. Some of them, Victor Kelly and Joe Momoney, were field trial winners. Others were sired by really great dogs which we did not own. Peggy, a slender black and white bitch, had a mother sired by Mr. Eugene M., who was himself sired by Eugene M. whom some consider the champion of them all. But often our best bred dogs have been outplayed by humbler ones whose distinguished ancestors may have been several generations behind.

Registered dogs, or non-registered dogs, what difference in the shooting field? If he is faithful, has bird sense and uses keen initiative in his plans and method of search, is strong and eager to please, these are the things that count. No human being would ever work this hard for you and if he is yours—you feed him and handle him—he perhaps thinks more of you than you do of yourself. If he is to be merely a hunting dog, and you do not plan to sell either him or his puppies for large sums, a slip of paper, a fancy name, will not better him except in the eyes of a judge.

Pointer or setter—that is a question. We must appreciate both for their separate qualities. For several years we acquired nothing except English setters. But now things have happened in the kennel. The favorites are two pointers. One of these is Mac, a large orange and white fellow with an inquisitive face and a pair of round friendly eyes the color of tangerines. "Mac would be an elegant looking dog," the handler once said of him, "if he only didn't have that crooked tail." But crooked tail or straight tail he comes to a point with as grand a manner, staunchly holding it for hours if necessary, as you would ever care to see. Mac is, besides, all but human and seems to understand in magical ways your words and gestures. He never gives in, and never potters; he never returns to the horses once he is afield, and casts out directly and independently to go about the business of his day. He is equally good with woodcock as with quail. And is absolutely insane about his chosen occupation—as you will see. He is all the more precious to us now because when he first came three years ago he not only jumped into coveys—when he imagined his handler was not watching—but proceeded to devour the first two birds shot over his back. But catch him making a mistake now? Never!

When morning dawns and the dew lies like white frost on the ground it is soon the hour to be off with one of these dogs, and to carry with you no cares in the world other than the correctness of your eye and behavior of the trigger finger. You will feel refreshed, if you came the day before from a city, or exhilarated if you live here every day. As you enter the room where an enormous breakfast before blazing logs awaits you, the austere heads of two Arctic walrus gaze down upon the scene with an expression of superciliousness. They may look a little inquisitive, those upright ridiculous faces out of each of which grow two white tusks; but as a matter of fact they are merely disdainful of rolling green fields, and trees, that they catch sight of through windows; not half as beautiful, they think, as blue water and white ice.

And you will wonder how they like the cheery call of the Bob White as compared to the shriek of the Arctic tern.

This large breakfast will add the finishing touch of confidence in yourself and a sense of well-being. For—"Life is pleasant. Life is good. The mere process of life is satisfactory"—says Virginia Woolf, and the process of it holds lovely moments like home-made sausage and fried apples and cakes from buckwheat ground by an old stone mill, and a polite servant who speaks to you in his soft low drawl about stuffed eggs and cold turkey sandwiches that he will "carry out" at noon.

Over wool shirts, for though the day may be warm, the evening will cool suddenly, you will wear a white drill hunting jacket, like the red cap of the deer hunter safer than khaki which fades into the autumn background. You will carry your own well-cherished gun, and I, the faithful twenty-gauge Remington pump using the twenty-six-inch barrel. If it be early in the season we will bring number nine shot; later in the year when birds are stronger and wilder, number eight; and always *chilled shot.*

Everything is in readiness, the horses and the stable boy, but as it happens the handler has not yet arrived with the dogs. This is unusual. Ordinarily he stands outside the gun room, waiting.

Quail at "Glenwild"

When we reach the kennel we might learn that Mac has jumped the nine-foot wire enclosure of his runway and is nowhere to be found. . . .

"He's de jumpinest dawg I evah did see," laughed Little Orange one morning when this actually occurred, as he tried to apologize, but you could see that the erring dog who cared so much for the fine sport of hunting was a favorite with the colored boy as well as with us. The handler raised his gun in the air and shot one shell. A few seconds later, from the field where he had stolen off to hunt alone, Mac appeared. He had not been taken out the preceding day, nor the day before, and apparently could not bear it any longer. He had been missing too many golden opportunities to find those feathered beauties whose scent so intrigued him.

Mac came trotting casually towards his handler, looked over the guns and men and horses—having perhaps figured he had better hurry back when he heard the shot but not quite certain the hunt would include him—and ambled off a trifle sheepishly to join his setter companions restlessly awaiting to be off.

"Does this happen often?" some one inquired of the handler.

Leighton smiled, "Well," he drawled, a slow twinkle in his eye, " . . . not so often, but quite often when we don't give him enough huntin'. Sometimes it gets so bad we have to tie a ball and chain on him to keep him home nights. . . ."

Through tall fields of broom sedge we went this day, Mac, Major a large and garrulous Llewellin, Peggy, and Pal who always reminds me of a wise old man. He never gets excited, never displays any unusual emotion—his hazel eyes give the impression of having seen all there is to see—except when the hunters delay too long at their lunch, then he commences to bark and demand that they hurry. Major and Pal were to stay with us during the forenoon while Mac and Peggy were to be tied in a negro's yard until time for the afternoon hunt.

The sun shone warm and delicious. Crimson sumach waved at us from fence rails, and all round us spread the coppery yellow of sedge, the green of pines, and we breathed that familiar fragrance of burning pine-logs so peculiar to the Southland. Negro cabins dotted here and there, offered us their porches overflowing with laughing children and their yards with chickens, stray dogs, and an occasional hog. Crops were picked so the fields were bare of yield.

The morning proved to be Major's. It had not been often that this bigger dog could outwit Pal. Out of the first nine coveys Major claimed six.

On his second find it took him several points to pin the birds that were all this time—so we discovered later—travelling along the ground ahead of his nose. When he froze for the seventh time we thought him still a bit uncertain and not one of us courted the effort, perhaps again unnecessary, of jumping down off the horses. We were tired of false alarms. So we chatted a few seconds about what we considered the chances of there actually being birds this time. When, to our disgust—and Major's—a large covey of about eighteen rose from under the dog's nose and sailed across the breadth of the corn field. Words could not describe our feelings. Not one gun even loaded!

Ten minutes later when the same dog pointed once more his handler leaned over his saddle and said: "I'd hate to tell old Major he's prevaricatin' again. I'm goin' to git off anyway—and mighty quick!"

Major was not prevaricating. A good-sized covey got up between us and the dog who had gone into the point in a sidewise fashion, his nose turned well around, his warning. And when three birds fell he stood there, steady, until he heard the familiar *Daid*, Major, *Daid*, Pal," and off they scurried to retrieve.

I am glad of Major's one day of victory over Pal, whose actions in the field are always experienced and competent, because Major's record, though he was sired by an imported Llewellin, had not been as good. And Major died not long afterward from some strange malady no one could name.

The afternoon was nearly as fruitful of coveys as the morning, twenty-eight birds in all, a good fare for Sunday dinner. The last covey was flushed in a sorghum field. Dusk had fallen before we had rounded up the singles in thickets and brier patches and along the edge of a stream where quicksand detained us from crossing just anywhere we would have wanted. Mac had carried himself in his usual independent manner "running off by himself certain he's going to find the birds" as some one remarked. While Peggy kept up her own end of the day with three or four coveys and several good honorings of her brace mate's finds. Peggy's ancestor, after all, was Eugene M.

As we climbed back on our mounts, tired in every muscle, but pleasantly so, we heard from all about us in the increasing darkness the scatter call of the Bob White quail. *Ka—loi—kee.* . . . *Ka —loi—kee* came the faint notes from first a plum thicket, then a brier patch. And who could refrain from pulling in his reins and stand still while watching these birds rise out of the ground and fly off to some chosen sanctuary. Before many more minutes the little gang would be together again, all that had not fallen to the gun, and in a solid round formation no larger than the rim of a plate, a formation that affords warmth and instant readiness to spring at the approach of danger.

For eight solid hours we had had no thoughts other than the fields and woods, the possible whereabouts of birds, the dogs, and even the horses who have, after many such seasons, learned to coöperate in an astonishingly intelligent manner. We turned now, the dogs trudging tiredly by our sides, through lanes of mud between ghostly armies of battered corn and cotton stalks. A three-mile ride lay ahead. Complete darkness came with a star or two in the sky. It was strange and mysterious riding that evening through dark silent cotton fields which had yielded a bumper crop and were now asleep. Yet it was not those wet slumbering fields which were most mysterious. For we were passing tiny, isolated cabins, shadows lying between perhaps two gaunt trees. They were small oases in the desert of last fall's crops. No children stood on the porches now and waved to us, for through the windows shone the fitful pinkish glow of a fire on every hearth. And as we rode by we glanced within and saw a roomful of black faces, black heads, black forms—all sizes—silhouetted against the walls where a reflection of red flames danced. Close to the fire they sat, munching on their frugal meal.

I thought of the scene in *Porgy,* inside the house, on the wild night when rang the dreaded hurricane bell. I thought of it more when we caught, in the cool still air, the sound of distant voices singing. The wavering shadows, though, were the only reminder. For those lighted cabins in cotton furrows did not offer a foreboding of tragedy. Instead we witnessed a great peace and contentment. Dogs barked lazily as we trotted by; soft voices called them back; children lay asleep in the arms of women near the crude family hearths where pine logs flickered.

XII

"Mary"

JANUARY TWENTY-FIRST, ten days before the closing of one more shooting season, turned out to be
a red-letter day for the *Glenwild* kennels and myself. But, when most red-letter days dawn they
are as problematical as any other; they seem no
different; and it is often that the importance of
the day itself cannot be appreciated until judged
in retrospect. So it was with this particular
Thursday.

I had been invited to hunt with an official of the
Illinois Central Railroad who lived several miles
down the highway. We were to try a territory in
the hills, often spoken of in fiction as the "back
country." Here fields are poor and soil is red and
poor whites dwell either in utter isolation or in
small communities of unpainted shacks. Because
of the inaccessibility and the distance away Leighton Finney, the dog handler, suggested that we
hunt only half a day and take but two dogs, Jake
and Major. The others were resting in preparation for their master's arrival, accompanied by
guests, the following day.

The weather had been treating us to unusual

warmth most of the season which had been exceedingly pleasant in one way, but hard on the dog's noses, and often too hot to move very fast on foot in following up singles "over the next gully" or "down at the bottom of the ravine." On this day a temperature of seventy-five degrees Fahrenheit in the sun, with butterflies fluttering through the perfumed air of false spring in the kindly climate, and bees and grasshoppers darting towards you and veering off, rather served to give you spring fever. Made you think longingly of cool streams surging over rocks and the distant call of a loon. Cardinals had arrived and were busily occupied in the process of looking up a summer home. Even the pine woods held an unexpected new odor, the sweet strong scent of an orange grove. A strange fragrance to emanate from pine woods but commented upon as well by the two men.

Leighton, while we were motoring back into the red hills where Orange would be waiting with the three horses, talked to me of the dogs. Mac had gashed his right eye on a fallen twig and was out of the running for a day or so. Young Colonel, a new dog, to our disappointment was not yet ready, being too eager to hunt he often overlooked coveys, and Peggy was ill with a form of influenza or intestinal flu. We were short of dogs. There still remained three weeks of the shooting season and there were to be guests from the North over each week-end. "We sure need another dog, badly," Leighton said, "I kind 'a hoped I could trade the young dog, Colonel, for a more experienced animal. But I haven't had any luck."

An hour or so later we were mounted. Orange trailed behind on a piebald pony. "It's sure hard on the dogs' noses—these warm days," Leighton commented, already a trifle discouraged as he swung along on his long-legged black horse with a broad western saddle. The gay Indian trappings of his bridle dangled this way and that. Leighton had once been a cowboy on a Texas range. But being a dog handler on a quail preserve, and running a gas station in off season, he far preferred. He cared as much for any hunting dog as he would have—I dare say—cared for his own children if he had had any. "Sure hard on their noses today," he was repeating. And Mr. Mills, third member of the party, thought the same.

Jake and Major, our choice for the day, were appealing animals, both of them. I liked them in the same way I liked all the dogs. None of them belonged to me, nor did they display any special devotion to one person with the possible exception of their handler who gave them the most time and the most attention. Some day I hoped that I might have my own dog, that I myself might learn to handle him in the field, to go off alone with him. How exciting it would be! I wanted terribly to learn what it would be like to have a hunting dog consider me his very own mistress.

The weather being hot and still, following upon two days of beating rain, the birds, as usual, played tricks on us. No luck in the bottoms, we headed towards the rolling woodlands "over yonder." When we reached the woods, cool and pleasant, almost immediately we scared up two coveys both of which roared up at least fifty yards ahead of the dogs. Grouse-like creatures! Out of these two coveys our bag claimed, on the singles, but three birds, combination of bad luck and poor shooting. We had to do better. We must bring home not less than fourteen, one for every one at the children's table, as well as ours. Guineas, turkey, young pig, might be suitable for other meals, but Sunday it must be quail. These wood birds, as we call them, were tree-fliers. Mark them to a certain tall tree we would and there stand below it, like gaping country-bumpkins on their first visit to the tall buildings of a city, craning our necks backward and gazing upwards for several minutes into the confusing branches. But to no avail. We never spotted the small brown balls who undoubtedly were watching our every move since the minute our backs were turned and we walked away, off they would sail—to another tree, pleased, of course, at having once more out-smarted dog and man.

Major and Jake were leading us down into a hollow on the edge of the denser woods. They were both birding and we were in a quandary as to whether one of our singles had gone thus far. It seemed an impossibly long distance. Neither dog was behaving as though he thought the scent another covey. This bird had apparently pitched and run along the ground. At least, so we imagined. Or else why the uncertainty? Back and forth they went, sterns down, whipping their curly blanks along the edge of deep grasses, and out into the open, heads up. For several minutes they continued in this way. And we followed.

"Steady Maj!" Leighton called.

Then Jake broke and trotted on down to a spring at the bottom of the hill and threw his hot body into the cooling water, floundering in it up to his neck, lapping it up greedily with his tongue. It was a trying day for a setter. Major continued his search, casting out about fifty yards. Then he too broke.

"Reckon we'd best go on," the handler said. "They've both broke. I wish old Maj' would take a drink. It'd help his nose."

Jake leaped up out of his refreshing bath and started in our direction, shaking himself.

In the flash of an eye, he whirled and stiffened. Up went his tail. Major, hastening towards the spring, saw him. At a distance of a good thirty yards he froze, crouching, in an awkward sitting position, with both hind legs sprawled under him. A comical sight.

"One of Major's funny ones!" our Southern friend commented with a laugh. "I love to watch that old dawg point." As he spoke, when I too laughed at Major, I thought of a game of statues that I sometimes play with my children. Major was a distorted statue.

We walked up, first pushing in front of Major and then swinging over behind Jake. The larger animal still did not move a muscle.

We were almost on top of Jake.

Up flew one bird, a rustle of wings, and a peculiar soft, twittering sound. Again, as in wild ducks, I thought the whistling issued from its bill, but instead was made by the air rushing through the three outer primary feathers of its wings. The bird rose straight up, higher, still higher; then, unlike a quail, sideslipped like a Wilson's snipe, and straightened out, with great speed veering off to the right.

The gun on my right went off. The three of

us had been too surprised to shoot—instantly. By this time the strange whistling bird—I had considered his action as strange but the two more experienced men understood—had darted behind a tree.

The bird dropped. *"Daid,* Jake, *daid,"* his handler ordered in a tone of voice that made the command instantly familiar to both dogs. "It's a woodcock!" Leighton added with great excitement. "Good shot, Stanley!"

The gunner who had brought down the bird now waited for Jake to retrieve it. This was done and he leaned over, patted the dog, removed the feathered object the curly-haired animal had been mouthing so tenderly as he obediently trotted towards the hunter. Then the man walked back to us, with great care carrying the prize in his right hand. A woodcock is a rare and beautiful thing. "Look at him. Ain't he a beauty!" he cried, approaching me. "Evah eaten one? . . . Take him for yo' lunch pa'ty. He's worth foah of quail."

Black, brown, and grey, this dainty bird was indeed a beauty. But quail—grouse—woodcock— are all beauties. And this bird was, as well, a superb morsel served on toast.

The cock was now laid into a special pocket of our friend's khaki jacket. "You cain't find many woodcock round these heah parts like we used to,"

he said. "Mah goodness how fine they are!"
Oddly enough three woodcock were flushed on
our own land during the following week-end.
Had they always been there? We do not know.
For woodcock are mysterious, fickle little migratory birds, night travellers secretive as to their
migrations, and considered by many the most
precious of our North American game birds.

Pleased with our special and assorted bag we
forgot about our own thirst, the heavy clothes we
were wearing, the hot setters, and the fact that we
still did not have many quail. But Leighton did
remark that he wished we had a brace of fresh
dogs. The difficulty had been distance and the
rough impassable-by-motor ground we were covering. We had no way to bring other animals
with us and nowhere to leave the tired ones. This
was the country of the "poor whites," their red
soil and small crops, their dingy unpainted shacks
far isolated on hill tops and in deep valleys. A few
years ago my heart would have ached at the sight
of those dilapidated little homes and the barefoot
mothers and fathers and children whom we passed
in the fields. But this day I could hardly feel the
same way. They had a house to live in, they had
a huge fat hog wallowing in a small enclosure behind the chicken coop where a rooster and five or
six hens strutted in the sunlight, they had a mule

to work their cash crop of cotton and corn, they had sorghum for molasses, and a garden on each side the house. Children were thin but their voices held the unmistakable ring of happiness, they had a dog or two, and perhaps a young wiggly kitten for playmates. The sun was warm on bare little legs and arms and hair that had perhaps never been confined by a hat. This sun gave them what health they had, the sun and clean air.

"Only three quail and one woodcock," bemoaned our friend who had suggested this particular hunting territory and had arranged beforehand for permission to shoot. "That fella sure gave me the wrong steer about this heah place. T'aint no good—at all!"

However, before so very long Major and Jake found more birds. We now had eight and the day was wearing on. We sat under a lofty virgin pine and ate a sandwich apiece which we had stuffed into our pockets on leaving home, and three shiny red apples that half-way quenched our thirst. And of these three sandwiches we shared fifty-fifty with our grateful canine companions. While we sat there resting, and talking of hunting dogs, guns, wild life, and the trials of farming, I sifted through my fingers the sharp brown strong-scented pine needles and rubbed them inside my palms so I could sniff later the sweet strong odor they left. Squirrels capered over our heads along their verdant ladders, and song birds chirped. It was lovely and clean and pine-smelling and restfully beautiful. How happy I was not to be living in a great jangling skyscraper city where there would be no trees and only a few grey doves circling the Art Institute, and not enough jobs and homes for all.

We rose from the ground, refreshed. Major and Jake laid back their heads and barked, rubbing their eager bodies against our legs. They were pleased to be starting again. They did not seem in the least weary because they were big dogs, and in good condition.

Very disheartening it was when we hunted farther and raised no more quail. Far away from home we were. A long, long ride. And we were tired.

"Think we'd better turn back?" I queried of Leighton who knew the country, and knew how much more the dogs could stand. We would, of course, not be taking these two out again, once they were home, for at least two days.

"Reckon we had, ma'am," came my answer.

We rode onward a few yards.

"Heh!" sounded an unfamiliar command from the rear.

At that very instant a young liver and white

pointer bitch, she was small and lean enough to count every rib, had emerged from the very atmosphere itself, and stood close by the horses. So quietly she came, so unexpected, that she might have been the phantom of a dog. Not heeding the "Heh!" she commenced to trot along beside our mounts, quite happily, though she did, once or twice, peer back over her shoulder in order to make sure about something, or some one, behind her. Aphrodite never rose from out the waves in a more sudden and astonishing manner than appared this little brown and white dog.

"Mary, come heah!" reiterated the voice.

It was then we turned in our saddles to discover a thin, thinner even than Mary, youngish man in shabby blue jeans strolling down the dry hillside over which we had just passed, walking slowly, his fingers pulling at a long yellow weed. We reined in and stopped, waiting for him to catch up.

"Y'all huntin' birds?" he called, clipping his words in such a manner it was difficult to distinguish just what he had mumbled.

"You got any?" bantered Leighton good-naturedly as he swung round. "It don't seem so." He spoke with a slow drawl. Often when he spoke it was hard to distinguish any note that would have marked him as a Texas cowboy. The gentle South had already laid its hands on him. For she is contagious to all who live with her during any length of time.

"Your dawg any good?" Leighton continued.

"Y'em. . . . He's good dawg."

"Does she come to the whistle?"

"No'm, she nevah did heah whistle."

"Does she back?"

"No'm, she won't back."

"Does she flush the birds so they get up wild?"

"No'm, she don't flush."

The thin man continued tearing to pieces the long yellow weed which he held in his left hand.

"I'll show you birds," he offered in a friendly fashion, not raising his voice, not changing his expression. "I'll walk, you ride."

But he did not walk. This was too much to permit any one to do. He threw himself, at our insistence, onto Leighton's five-gaited steed, and settled himself on the slippery sweaty flanks of an old Dobbin who possibly wondered what had suddenly taken place. . . . On his back now sat two riders instead of one. Behind the western saddle dangled a pair of long skinny legs in shabby overalls and high black shoes with wide holes under the soles.

We approached the top of the next ridge. Mary was hunting wider, and fresher than either of the larger dogs who had been afield since morning.

"Birds hea'h!" the thin man with the pinched white face ejaculated, pointing at the same time with his right hand towards a vague location to the east of us. "Saw'm ye'terday."

The two setters had already covered the territory to which the man vaguely referred. On they had gone, neither of them birding.

"She'm got birds," we heard the man drawl laconically, "I kin tell how'm she look."

She?—Where was she? The three of us with guns had not attributed the slightest importance to Mary; it was Jake and Major on whom we still depended.

We found her, on the steadiest prettiest point you could ever wish to see. Not moving a muscle, right fore leg gracefully raised, tail straight, head up, the slim young bitch firmly held her stance.

Jake and Major caught the excitement. This strange little lady imagined she had found game in cover they had already examined. It must be a joke. "What does she mean by playing us such a trick?" Jake's black eyes seemed to demand though he wasted no time in honoring her point. It was pretty nervy for a lady to butt into a gentleman's business—in the way she had!

"She's got the birds, Ma'am." Leighton

drawled, his voice not doubting the little bitch. "Let's take them off the young dog first—even if those old dogs have birds too."

Burr-rr! Up they catapulted—but only three quail.

We all shot, three guns. Not one bird fell.

"I waited for the rest of the covey," some one admitted with a groan. So had we all. Then we all burst out laughing—all except the solemn man in overalls who pulled at his weed and said nothing. Our further chagrin came when we caught the heartfelt disappointment in the serious amber eyes of a thin young dog.

On we headed, towards the three birds who had separated and flown a good half-mile. This time our new-found friend chose to proceed on foot. Mary, his pointer, having forgiven us, in the way dogs do, now raced ahead with the eagerness of a greyhound, covering with care all possible bird-country as she went. We found one single and brought it down. Again it was Mary's find, as Jake and Major were working busily elsewhere. They were a pair of annoyed veterans of several years' experience, when they returned at the shot of the gun to find a bird grassed, and the small stranger in their midst the finder of the treasure.

Leighton's mind had been working. "Will you

trade your bitch for a setter puppy?" he called back over his shoulder to the man in overalls, referring to young Colonel as trade. "He'll be a fine dog by next fall."

"No'm—I won't trade her," replied Mary's owner.

A few minutes later as we were riding on, and our thin friend continued to say he preferred to walk, Leighton reopened the same subject.

"Will you trade her for the puppy—and five dollars?" (It must be remembered this was the end of the shooting season and hunting dogs have to be fed for nine and a half months before the return of another season.)

"No'm. I won't trade her fer nuthin'! I want to breed her fer pups." This was said quite decisively.

In the meantime we were making headway down off the wooded slope we had climbed. The soil was red and sandy. Our horses' hoofs clicked noisily against loose stones. It was growing late, would soon be sundown.

The thin figure in the blue jeans edged closer to us. Our mounts, anxious to start homeward, were being held down with some difficulty to a slow walk.

"I'll sell her fer cash—if you'll gimme one o' her pups!" he announced, finally, as if he had been thinking it over, and now snipped his lips on this new and sudden decision.

So it was that Mary, the little pointer, made her first visit to *Glenwild*. In the arrangements made between Leighton and this man who called himself Ed, Ed was to bring her there the following morning in plenty of time for the afternoon hunt. As I mentioned earlier, we sorely needed one more dog to carry us through the last two weeks. We were to try Mary and let him hear in a day or so what we thought of her and whether or not we intended keeping her. It had not been often that we had found good hunting dogs in the highways and byways and in such an unexpected fashion.

True to his word, at noon Ed stood by the plantation offices when the train whistled from the North. His little bitch on a ragged rope, the two of them stood there, waiting, wondering, and both bewildered by all that had happened. The dog was shivering and staring about her. The man's lowered eyes fastened themselves on his dusty shoes as though he, too, were too frightened to glance up.

"A dog for you to try this afternoon," I said to my husband as in the car we passed the thin man and thin little animal who still awaited instructions.

"A pointer?"

"Yes. It seems she comes from the same kennels, or her mother did, as Mac, your favorite dog."

"She's got good blood, then," commented the Master of *Glenwild*, only mildly interested, as on we hastened in order to change our clothes for the shooting field.

Mary accompanied a party of three, and the thin man commenced his seven-mile tramp homeward.

On this day Mary's bracemate was Pal, wise son of a field trial winner. Pal's steadiness and his unfailing quartering of every good-looking cover we figured would be helpful to a young and nervous eighteen-months-old puppy.

Almost at once Pal came to point on a covey in a plum thicket. Now came Mary's first big problem in the field. Heretofore, she had self-hunted, and wandered freely with chickens, pigs, and live stock; but never before had she seen another dog make a find and stiffen on birds. The day before—it had been *her* covey and the two big setters had been merely honoring her find.

"Steady, Mary!" her prospective master ordered, his voice as calm and steady as his command. For the Master of *Glenwild* is an excellent gentleman handler of dogs in the shooting field. He does it with quietness and firmness and tact. "Steady—little girl!" his voice came again. The three of us waited.

Mary glanced at him from the corner of one amber eye. It was as though she knew her big moment had come. It was as though she feared she would not rise to the occasion. Her instinct must have told her what was right but her reasoning might very well be wrong. She shivered, from her tail to her head. Then, suddenly something clicked. Perhaps she remembered the performance of Jake and Major the day before? Whatever it was, there where she stood, one eye still on the man whose voice had spoken to her and called her by name, she straightened out into a perfect stance comparable with the one she had assumed on her own birds the preceding afternoon. She had learned to honor another dog's point.

The birds got up. The guns blazed. Three birds fell.

But something had frightened her. In one lean bound Mary had covered the thickets, with never a care as to whether the birds were retrieved, and in due time had reached her old home, seven miles away. She reached it, before the return of her former master.

Honestly, my heart bled for the little animal.

"Mary"

We had so hoped she would do well. Just the day before she had had the nerve to outwit two old dogs in the field, and staunchly hold her point in the face of seeing that no one even believed her. In fact if dogs have a means of communication, Jake and Major, considering what she did, must have certainly told her plenty. She had interfered, had taken birds directly out from under their very noses, and she—a lady.

What had frightened her—this time? Was it the roar of the three guns so close over her body? Or was it the fear that, after all, she had done wrong? We will never know.

If she had only been human I could have said so much to her. Could have told her about the time I missed a polar bear. It wasn't the fact that I had missed the bear that counted now, but it was the fact that I had lacked a man's nerve in a bad pinch which griped me. So had poor half-starved little Mary. . . . She had, besides, lacked the nerve to stand by and receive her punishment —if punishment were due her.

The next morning the two of them, the thin man and the thin dog, were back. Mary on the end of the same ragged rope. Leighton had been instructed to pay "Ed" the price he had asked and we would try and use her during the ensuing three weeks. Accordingly, Mary was placed in the runway with the other female dogs, all setters. There we fed her and petted her, and she became less frightened, and less strained, and with relish devoured the new kind of dog food. She even commenced to take on weight. "Pot likker and scraps, Ma'am, is about all that little bitch ever had," Leighton commented as together one evening we watched her fall upon and avidly devour the balanced ration. "She ain't never seen a bone before. Watch her!—She all but claws it to pieces."

A few days later Mary went again into the shooting field and once more with Pal. We all wondered what she would do. It's a man's world, and a hard world, little Mary, and if you don't do well this time—but we couldn't tell her. She wouldn't understand. So we crossed our fingers— and hoped.

The instant we had splashed across the first branch and entered a cotton patch, the young creature pulled out ahead of the horses, raced across the muddy furrows with the self-confidence and speed of a field trial performer. It was thrilling to watch her go. Never once waiting on Pal nor basing her decisions on his, Mary quickly decided for herself in which cover or thicket she cared to hunt, and thereupon leaped into briers where older and heavier dogs never could penetrate.

Though, until the day she ran for home, she had never heard a dog whistle, today she watched Pal's philosophic and immediate surrender to it. As well she studied the accompanying signals from a man's arm, and with quick obedience, she turned.

Once we lost her. On birds we found her in a thicket so dense we could not follow. Previously to locating her we had blown the whistle and called and shouted her name, but with no success.

"You can't blow that little bitch off birds!" Leighton shouted with glee, as though he were a small boy showing off a find. "I sure wish Mister Borden could see her now. She'll be one of the best dogs we've ever had!"

Nor would she move when she found more birds and the guns roared and the birds fell. Steadily, unflinchingly, she stood her point.

She had known no training. Nor had she had any previous experience with men and dogs in search of quail. She had been a one-man dog, a lone hunter who knew no signals, nor the art of following commands. Yet in no time she had learned. I cannot help but puzzle, every now and then, when looking into those clear amber eyes whether her failure that day ever worries Mary now. For in ten days she was already a star performer, taking into consideration, of course, her youth, her shyness, and her initial timidity in this new way of hunting birds. Never more now did she make a serious mistake. Fortunate Mary! She "had had it in her," the men now agree.

Several days after the shooting season had closed, the thin man in the same shabby overalls trudged down the dusty road towards the offices of *Glenwild*. He stopped for a moment in front of the white, red-roofed gas station where Leighton had once more become a business man. "Howdy, Ed?" Leighton called.

Ed waited a few moments before responding. He seemed nervous, afraid to ask the question that hung on his lips. Instead he commenced to pull at a hangnail on one of his thumbs.

"There's a letter here for you, Ed." Leighton stepped out from under the canopy and handed him a letter.

Ed looked at it. It was white and small and had a red line bordering the flap. "Letter?" he murmured, and then closed his lips on the word as though he shouldn't have spoken. "Letter?" he repeated, "Fer me?"

"Yes. Open it."

Reluctantly his fingers plucked at the flap and managed to get it unsealed. He pulled forth the

Glenwild stationery, unfolded it, stared at it. He continued to stare at it—but said nothing.

Leighton decided to glance over his shoulder. The writing on the paper was being held upside down.

"Shall I read it for you, Ed?"

The man's hands trembled ever so slightly——

"Ye'm," he said, and tightly shut his lips.

"Well, then, first take a look inside the envelope—before I do."

The man turned his head and stared at Leighton. But this time his dark fleeting eyes had changed their expression. Hadn't Leighton suggested something about "looking inside the envelope"—?

So he jabbed one thin finger down into the paper depths as though it had been a prong, and jerked into view a roll of greenbacks. He took an involuntary step forward, as though he weren't quite certain of his balance.

"Money!" he grunted aloud, his tell-tale face lighting with the suddenness of an electric globe turned on in the midst of utter darkness. "Money —fer me?"

"Yes—they liked your little bitch so well they're giving you more than you asked. . . . You see she's the first huntin' dog the Missus ever owned for herself. She's crazy about her and going to learn how to handle her herself—so's she—" But Ed had walked away.

A few hours later Leighton said to me, "It didn't occur to me, ma'am, that he would think your letter would say you folks didn't want to keep Mary—after all this time—and wanted to send her back. He must 'a needed the money awful bad. . . . I wish you could've been there to've seen his face as he walked away."

Mary is mine. Still thin, and always a trifle high strung, she is nevertheless a straight thinker, a tireless worker, and a loyal friend.

I am glad that this new way of living has brought one more person closer to the appreciation of nature and its great beauties, of wild life, and to the better understanding and enjoyance of humble, human contacts far removed from that which pertains, or is judged by, worldly aims and worldly successes.

Rich man, poor man, begger man, thief, what difference in the trout stream or shooting field? None. Only the comparison in technique and fair play . . . with fish in our streams and birds in our fields—yes—civilization must be safe.

Appendix

WHAT IS BEING DONE AT GLENWILD PLANTATION TO
PRESERVE AND PROPAGATE THE BOB WHITE QUAIL

This plantation has to take into consideration the needs of sixty tenant families, their crops, their cattle, hogs, and domestic pets—all detrimental to the nesting of Bob White. When we tractor-farmed, the fields being kept large and wide in order that the machines need not constantly turn, quail were scarce. Now, that we might increase their growth, we have reverted to the "old-fashioned Mississippi-style of farming" as some one aptly expressed it. The tenant farmers, black or white as the case may be, with their one mule and hand plow outfit, avoid the thicket and brier patches rather than clear them out. Briers are now saved as cover for birds, and plum thickets for nests. Cultivated fields are smaller. The manager allots land to be worked by each tenant, and round those smaller fields now rise patches of ragweed, sedgebroom, lespedeza, partridge pea, and other leguminous plants, providing feed, dusting, and roosting places. Feed patches must be in close proximity to cover, cover to water, and so on. For these gallinaceous birds seldom fly, unless flushed, from one cover to another but walk instead like a brood of guineas or chickens, hugging closely to some protection always on the lookout for danger. As the elements will alter their habits of the previous several days and shift their course of travel, so also will the exhaustion of existing food in one location and the plentifulness of it in some other.

In spring and summer cattle and mules are pastured in low places, and there keep down the tall grass where it is not suitable for quail to nest, because of big rains that would wash away nests and young. Birds, not realizing this, would otherwise prefer these locations because of their lushness and nearness to some "branch." When autumn comes, and crops are picked, and young birds grown, livestock is again turned out in order that they may beat down the luxuriant cover of six-foot sedge grass, and clean out brier thickets too dense even for birds. . . . Of course, there are always the high woodland areas that are resorted to by the birds in a wet season and that ever remain a favorite haunt for a good many coveys where "mast" from the various oaks, sweet gums, and pine, and seeds of the flowering dogwood, and cherry, fill their crops.

When sedge broom grows too heavy we turn it under, seed it with sweepings from hay-lofts, and the fields come up the first year in lespedeza, buttonwood, ragweed, and such, offering food and excellent cover. Besides explaining to the tenant the need of keeping tied-up all domestic animals from the first of April until July—cats being the worst enemy of quail and quail's eggs and the hardest to regulate—we supply each farmer with peas to grow along with their corn. Each farmer must plant a good-sized patch of sorghum which when cut for molasses leaves the tops as another food, and the sorghum itself serves as a place for dusting.

Concerning the natural enemies of quail, the varmint and the hawk, these two remain a problem. Several years ago we trapped, in spring when leaves were first appearing on the trees, owls and hawks. But now we do it no longer since we caught mostly the hawks who do

more good than harm—eating snakes, rats, insects, etc.
—and seldom found trapped the one we wanted, the
sharp-shinned hawk so harmful to quail. Yet we do
wage a war on o'possums, raccoon, mink, skunks, and
bobcats. During winter fur hunters are permitted to
hunt with packs of hounds; and in spring we burn out
suspicious looking cover where bobcats and red fox
abound. A prominent Kentucky sportsman is reputed
to have cut down all persimmon trees—being the best
food of coons and possums—on his vast preserve and
attributes this as much as anything else to the large number of coveys found on his land. We may try this—
yet, though at the present writing we have a world of
birds.

Despite all these faithful precautions in order to
increase the numbers of a game bird who should be
saved for generations to come, when an abnormally
rainy spring and summer takes place, through no fault
of man or beast the nests are drowned out in wholesale
destruction.

Bibliography

Classics of the American Shooting Field—Edited by JOHN C. PHILLIPS AND LEWIS WEBB HILL, M.D.
Upland Game Bird Shooting in America—DERRYDALE PRESS.
Upland Game Birds—SANDYS and VAN DYKE.
A Sportsman's Scrapbook—JOHN C. PHILLIPS.
The Bob White Quail—HERBERT L. STODDARD.
The Water Fowl Family—SANFORD, BISHOP and VAN DYKE.
Jack Miner and the Birds—JACK MINER.
Tales of Rod and Gun—Compiled by HARRY McGUIRE.
Wild Game—Its Legal Status—Two Pamphlets.
How to Train Your Bird Dog—HORACE LYTLE.
Twentieth Century Bird Dog Training and Kennel Management—E. M. SHELLEY.
Lives of Game Animals—ERNEST THOMPSON SETON.
Dumb-Bell of Brookfield—JOHN TAINTOR FOOTE.
Sporting Rifles and Rifle Shooting—JOHN CASWELL.
Hunting in Alaska and The Arctic—SCULL.
How to Shoot—ROBERT CHURCHILL.
The American Rifle—WHELEN.
The Still Hunter—VAN DYKE.
The Book of Woodcraft—ERNEST THOMPSON SETON.
Camping and Woodcraft—KEPHART.
Life of Myton—NIMROD.
Memo—Go Fishing—BOB BECKER.
The Fine Art of Fishing—SAMUEL G. CAMP.
Salmon and Trout—DEAN SAGE . . . and others.

Bibliography

The Wedding Gift—John Taintor Foote.
A Short History of Mississippi—James K. Hosmer.
Heaven Trees—Stark Young.
The Outlaw Years—Robert M. Coates.